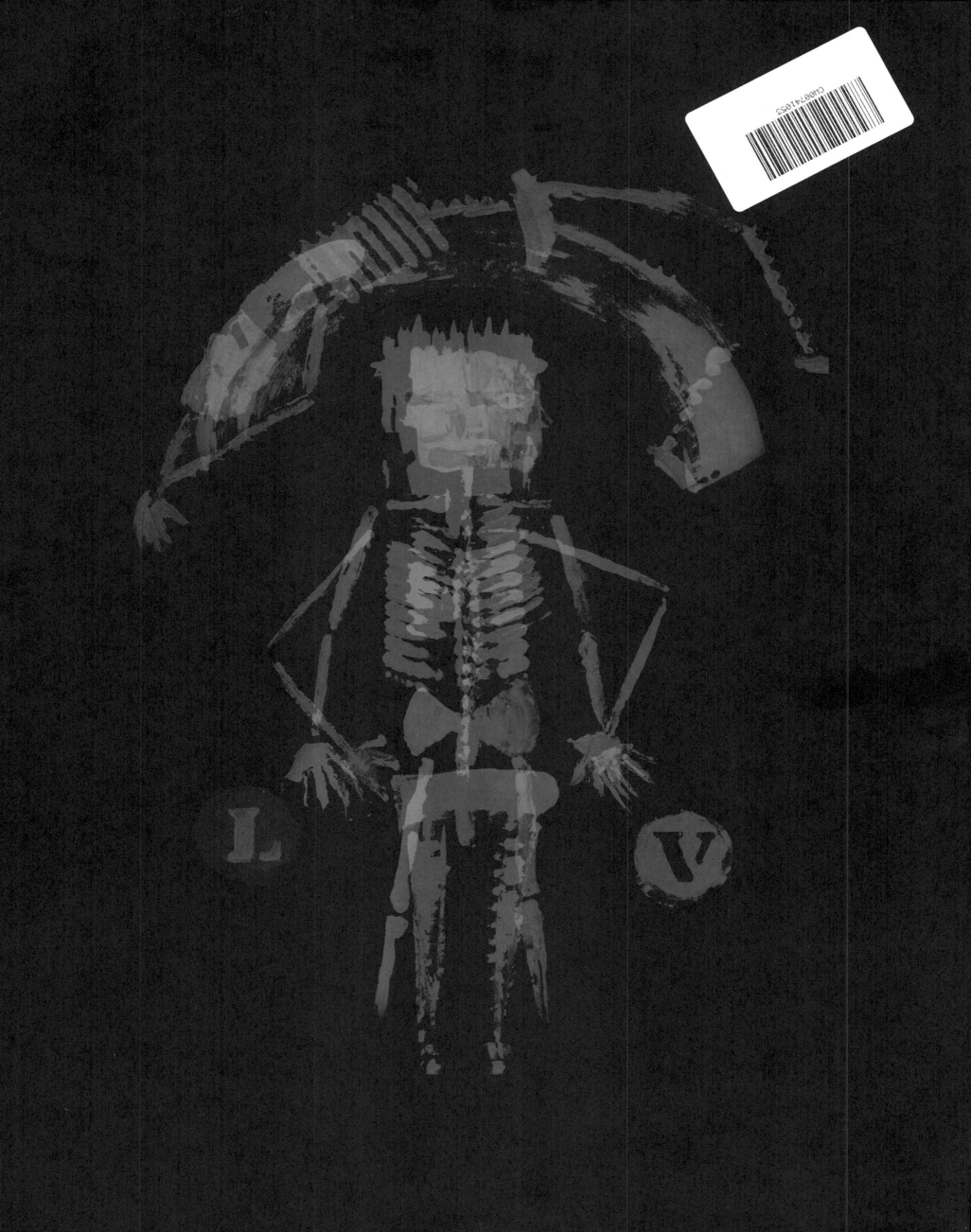

DREAM

DREAM

A Journal by Larry Vigon

THE QUANTUCK LANE PRESS

NEW YORK

I would like to thank the following people for making this book possible:
Ricky Jay, Jim Mairs, J. Marvin Spiegelman, Paul Wang, Michael Kim, Janet Muff, Hugh Milstein,
Ronn Brown, Anna Bolek, Brook Wilensky-Lanford, Steve Woodall and my wife, Sandra.

Dream: A Journal
Larry Vigon

Printed in Italy
First Edition
The text of this book is composed in: Stempel Garamond
With the display set in: Stempel Garamond
Composition and book design by Larry Vigon and Paul Wang,
Manufacturing by Mondadori Printing, Italy

ISBN: 1-59372-018-1

The Quantuck Lane Press, New York
www.quantucklanepress.com

Distributed by: W.W. Norton & Company, 500 Fifth Avenue, New York, NY 10110
www.wwnorton.com

W.W. Norton & Company Ltd., Castle House, 75/76 Wells Street, London, WIT 3QT

1 2 3 4 5 6 7 8 9 0

For Sandra

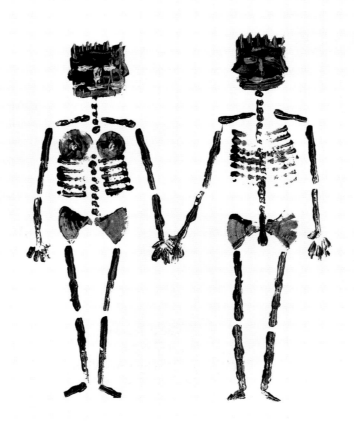

For the past fifteen years I have been writing down my dreams and accompanying them with painted images that directly illustrate a dream or just bubble up from the unconscious. The process is for me both therapeutic and meditative. There is something about the act of dipping a pen into ink, the sound of the pen scratching the paper, and the application and layering of paint that brings clarity to my thoughts and feelings. In the bringing together of dream and paint, imagination and matter, both are changed. More importantly, I am changed in an alchemical process that turns fear and anxiety into a creative, healing, and life-affirming activity.

In the beginning, this deeply personal journey into the unconscious was exclusively for self-exploration and understanding. As time passed, however, the journals took on a life of their own. Gradually, I began to show them to other people and was surprised that nearly everyone wanted to touch the images, something that is not usually encouraged with a piece of art. Yet these very textured and tactile paintings begged to be explored through touch as well as vision. Just as working manually with image and matter brought greater depth to my own experience, so, too, I realized, touching the material image added another layer of depth to the viewer's experience.

It also became apparent that my work ignited the creative spark in others, inspiring them to start their own journals. This was a by-product that surprised and delighted me. Given today's reliance on computers, some artists have abandoned ink and paint and pens and brushes for the screen and keyboard; they no longer have a hands-on relationship with the age-old artistic materials and so became disconnected from the organic pace at which creativity unfolds. I have found in my own work that keeping a journal provides an important balance to what has been lost in our technological era.

At the time of this writing I am coming to the end of my eighth journal, each one of which has taken about a year and a half to complete. This way of working with dreams and imagination has become an integral part of my life. My wish in producing this book, then, is to inspire others to create their own journals, whether through writing, painting, or collaging with photos or found objects—to see journaling not as an alternative to technology but as an adjunct.

Introduction

Larry Vigon has asked me to present a brief introduction to this evocative book of paintings and drawings, the result of his many years' work with dreams. The story begins when Larry came to me for analysis, having been overwhelmed by a nameless anxiety that was indeed close to dread. To Larry, an otherwise well-functioning, creative, and gifted man, these feelings were shocking, of course, but to me, a Jungian analyst, this was not an unusual event. It suggested an impending eruption of unconscious contents, all pressing to be "seen" and "heard," and, psychologically speaking, to be assimilated and integrated.

Knowing the author's great gifts as an artist, which were happily geared to commercial art and design, I suggested that he confront this invasion from the unconscious by giving it form through his artistic and imaginative capacity. He eagerly assented and there followed many years of significant and powerful paintings. These were intended only for his own inner development but, occasionally, they proved fruitful for his work in design. After some years, Larry felt the need to include his written dreams in picture/dream books, and in this way he came to unite both word and image.

Larry also worked analytically in the usual way, dealing with dreams, fantasies, and day-world experiences. After several years, he discontinued analysis but returned occasionally for further periods of psychological work. Throughout the years, he remained faithful to this visual and sensory (many of the works have a tactile element in them, too) mode of connecting with his soul, not only during his daily life but also during weekend "vacations" and time spent in his beloved Italy. All of this work has contributed to his inner development.

Many readers in our psychological age will be familiar with this use of artistic materials as part of a psychotherapeutic or analytic process but, still, a word of historical background might be useful.

In the nineteenth century, it was not uncommon for people in mental asylums to paint on their own, something their doctors believed was helpful to them. In the main, though, these works made little sense with regard to the rationalist, nonpsychologically oriented spirit of the time. There are several fathers and mothers of the use of art in psychotherapy, but the one who has been most impressive (at least to a Jungian analyst like myself) was C. G. Jung. Around 1912, Jung found himself pathetically adrift after a painful but necessary parting from his mentor and colleague Sigmund Freud. No longer connected to the Christianity of his family, nor contained in the rationalist myth propounded by his colleagues, Jung felt he had no myth at all. He decided, therefore, to let the psyche (unconscious) speak for itself and hit upon the idea of returning to the sand and water play of his childhood. Working in this way, he constructed whole villages, and, indeed, it was this use of sand and water that ultimately took on a life of its own (via Jung's pupil Dora Kalff) to become the world-famous sandplay method of therapy.

As a result of this play with sand and water, Jung gradually began to draw and paint the powerful images that came to him in dream and fantasy. Then he began to dialogue with the figures from the unconscious when they had a mind to so communicate. These activities, which lasted several years, were foundational for Jung, and he said that all of his later discoveries regarding the psyche had their origins in this work. He called this method of actively communicating with unconscious figures "active imagination."

Out of such work, the entire field of art therapy ultimately emerged, and many disciplines now make use of such methods. Jung, however, was careful to see his work not as art but as an adjunct to healing. Marie-Louise von Franz, Jung's last and perhaps most gifted pupil, used to say that one should paint or write "for the desk drawer," the point being that lack of artistic skills was no hindrance to psychological work. In my own life, at the end of my eight-year Jungian analyses, I felt called upon to do a series of watercolors, which illustrated my own myth quite satisfactorily. Since then, I have made good use of both art and writing in my personal work and also with patients.

Working with professional artists, however, raises a different question. Jung thought it best if such people simply did their psychological artwork with the nonfavored hand. I have had a different view. I have found that when artists work on their inner images for the sake of psychological development a subtle but distinct, dimension becomes active. This was the case with Larry Vigon. He adapted with alacrity to this "other" use of his imagination and skills, which served his own soul and in the process of psychological transformation. Since he was not conflicted about this noncommercial activity, he could throw himself into it fully. My own stance was simply to receive and be touched by his work, making a comment or two but rarely interpreting his dreams and fantasy material in the customary analytic way.

As this book shows, the method seems to have produced marvelous results. Although the reader might want an elaborate interpretation of the years-long process illustrated in the following pages, it is Larry's, as well as my own, preference to let the work speak for itself.

It is a pleasure and honor for me to accompany Larry Vigon in this presentation of his deep work to a larger audience.

I got out of my car. I was wearing tennis whites but I was not going to play tennis I think I was going to New York. There was a young Mexican guy there. He said are you getting this car in that green color. I said no this is it, pointing to my blue car. I was trying to close the trunk but my tennis bag kept getting in the way. Then from a room a man looked out at us and asked me to come inside and talk. He had heard me talking to the Mexican guy. The Mexican needed to buy something but couldn't find it. I think it was something for gardening work. I knew where to buy such a thing. in fact. I remember thinking it was pretty easy to purchase one of the devices. The man inside was Eastern European, a big man with a mustache. There was another man in the room also Eastern European but very tall at least seven feet. I remember looking up at him in amazement the other man commented on how big he was. They also needed this device. I think they were all one family. I was trying to explain where to buy this thing but it was getting very complicated with gathering the rest of his family, dropping his mother off on Melrose, driving long distances. I didn't understand why this was such an involved family project. Then the wife of the very tall man came into the room. She was a very attractive Black woman. She told me the real problem was people didn't want to do business with them because she was Black and her family foreign. I was in total disbelief that in this day and age people still had a problem with this sort of thing.

I was sitting with Brad Pitt, he was my analyst. As we talked a group began to gather (for a group session) I only knew of them; a guy named Leon (we didn't talk). I didn't like the group session and was glad when it was over. After the group left I had a lot of stuff to clean up and put away. I felt uneasy taking so much time. I felt as if Brad wanted me to stay. I remember throwing a white t-shirt into a room and startling a girl talking to Brad. It seemed I couldn't finish streightning things out (cleaning-packing etc.)

I was walking somewhere I don't know. I touched my right hand to my left and I noticed I was wearing my wedding ring. I didn't remember putting it on but I felt good it was there.

I was at the beach with Brian Walton and Jon Poctor. Brian had a strange boat for playing in the surf. It seemed to be made of steel tubes and canvas. He attempted to get out through the surf but was not successful even though the water was very calm and the waves quite small. A small wave had knocked him over and he came ashore and said You try it. I thought no problem. I'm a ex surfer this is a piece of cake. As I paddle out using my hands because Brian had the paddle a bigger than usual wave appeared. Brian and Jon thought I was going to get creamed but I knew the technique to get through. Brian and Jon were impressed. Then the ocean changed. The surface became rough and the waves bigger. The waves were too big for this strange boat. It was very frustrating because I knew if the ocean was the way it was when Brian was in the water I could get some good rides and really show them how its done. I knew exactly how to do it but the conditions preventing me from doing it were out of my control.

I was in a restaurant I had to pee. In the middle of the room was a bowl on a wooden stand. It was a metal bowl with some design on it. As I stood at the bowl I was aware of everyone looking at me, even though it was the place for people to pee. I was not able to pee and kept trying to cover my cock with my hands.

I was meeting Roland Young for a game of tennis when we arrived at the tennis club I realized I had forgotten all of my tennis clouthes and racket I told Roland to wait while I went to the pro shop to buy new stuff. I asked the pro shop employee for Nike and he said they didn't have any. I said I wanted the Nike clouthes like Pete Sampras wears. He was no help, he showed me another design. It had long sleeves. I said it's too hot for long ~~sleeve~~ sleeves I already have a long sleeved sweatshirt on. I remember not having the right shoes then having the right shoes. I don't remember where this dream went but it was frustrating.

I was lying on my bed. The bed was outside. The gardner was there working in the backyard. He was a middle aged Mexican man, dark and weathered looking. He spoke no English. I noticed as he was watering the flowers next to the bed that he had tied three hoses together but only had the water pressure at a minimum. I wondered why he would have all this capability but only use a fraction of it. I closed my eyes to go to sleep. I did not feel uncomfortable doing this with the gardner working around me.

I was sitting on a stone bench with my partner David. It was in a corridor in a Cambodian like temple. We were talking and looking out of a large window in the stone wall. I said look! there's a monkey, then there were more monkies. The longer we looked the more we saw. There were birds and other animals playing in the jungle outside the window. Then a man walked by us dressed in a business suit. As he passed me I said Hello but he did not respond. When I looked at him again he was still walking away from me but he was facing me. His face changed to a face of another man then a ~~wom~~ woman as he disappeared into the darkness of the corridor. Very eerie.

A gypsy man asked me to dance with him. I agreed and went over to him. He put his arm around mine and we began to dance arm in arm. Then he took out a knife and cut my arm. I remember it was an ugly cut, small but the shape was rough and the blood was dark. Then he touched the cut with his finger and began touching my arm in other spots up closer to my hand. Everywhere he touched left a duplicate cut. We continued to dance around in a circle. There were other gypsys also dancing. Then he took out a long needle like

device and wanted to stick it through my wrist. At first I was very much against this idea but as I thought about it I decided that if I was going to do this dance at all, I had to do it all the way. So I let him stab my wrist with the needle. To my surprise it did not hurt.

September 1997
Miramar Hotel Room #620
Montecito

There was a party given in my honor. Most of the guests ~~were~~ were black. Of the many people in ~~the attendance~~ attendance only a few were white. There ~~was~~ a large dish with white maccaroni and something else like dark rice (maybe) ● some kind of dark colored food. I kept trying to push the two different colored foods together. There was not enough dark food to mix and I remember requesting more of the dark or black colored food.

Quincy Jones was in a parking lot. I was pulling in the lot and saw a pair of sun glasses or regular glasses I'm not sure. The were thick framed black glasses. I avoided running over them. Quincy Jones was disappointed I missed them. They were his old glasses and he had just purchased some new ones. The new glasses were ~~much~~ much more elligant and contemporary. Now I am driving a big Cadallac, my father and mother are passengers. I remember some ugly colorful houses. We ~~are~~ are back at the parking lot. Quincy Jones is still there and so are the glasses on the ground. This time I say, don't worry I'll get them this time. As I try to run over the glasses they just get knocked into a place I can't get to them.

I was being chased by a werewolf. After a long time I became fed up with the situation. I stopped and confronted th werewolf and then I became the werewolf. I seemed to change from the classic Wolfman of the old films to a human with the head of a real wolf. I remember feeling good in this form. I was in control of the werewolf spirit ~~and~~ and able to keep from being mean spirited.

I was at home but it looked more like a farmyard outside. I went into a shack like building. As I was looking around inside this shack I felt the urge to urinate. At first I was just going to pee on the floor but then I noticed there was a toilet in the room just there, no inclosure. I went over to the toilet, I saw it had not been cleaned or even flushed for a while. As I urinated into the toilet flames shot up as if I had caused some kind of reaction in the mess in the toilet. I also realized that I could put the fire out with my urine. So it was a series of fires and me putting out fires. At the same time I was doing this I could see my neighbor Frances. She saw me inside the shack and waved I hoped she couldn't see me peeing.

I was buying a house in Umbria. It was a typical fixer-upper but there was a beautiful big view and you could see an old town just a five minute drive from the house.

Sam had to have an emergency operation. I think Dr. Heller was going to do the surgery. The problem was that no one had a scalpel. But I just happened to have a whole kit ful of them. I opened up the kit to reveal several scalpels with a assortment of blades. I went into the room where the surgery was going to take place. Sam was on a table, a sheet covered her. She sat up to speak with me. The sheet fell and she was naked. I thought to myself, I thought her tits would be bigger.

I was a policeman. I don't remember the first part of this dream. I went over to a girls house. In the living room were two boys maybe six or eight years old. I asked them where is (I can't remember her name) They said upstairs in her room. I went upstairs We were very happy to see eachother. I know we kissed. I was a passionate relationship. Then we heard a noise downstairs. She said quick get out of here, its my father. I ran down the hall or stairs but realized I had forgotten my hat. I ran back to her room, she handed me the hat and I ran down the stairs to the livingroom. The kids had gone to bed all the lights were out. I could see the shadowy bizure of the girls father standing near the door. Then I woke up feeling frightened.

I was at Tommy Steele's house. I said something about his swimming pool. He said he didn't have a pool. I my mind I could see the pool as if I had been there before I went out to his backyard where I remembered the pool was but it was all cement. I looked closely at the cement I could see the cracks were old. Then we were sitting together on the side of Tommy's pool. I swam a couple of laps but I was surprised that I swam so poorly knowing I such a good swimmer. I wanted to do a racing dive and really put some effort into a couple of really good strong laps. I could see in my mind how well I should be swimming. Then we were sitting at the other end of the pool. Tommy was reading something. I lifted the filter cover. Inside were several cats and a bird. the bird was only a few days old. Tomm gave it some food on the tips of his finger. One cat he said had some kind of ho on its head I didn't want to pet it eventhough I couldn't see anything. One of the kittens was actually a tiger. I said to Tommy I had to keep pee ering you but tell me about this one He thats — he's like one of the family. Then I was raising my own three day old bird a sparrow or finch. He grew up very peathy but could not bear to be without me around at all times. I had to take him to work and call every day from Italy so he could hear my voice. Sam said I really helped. I couldn't take him to Italy with me.

looked like an olive

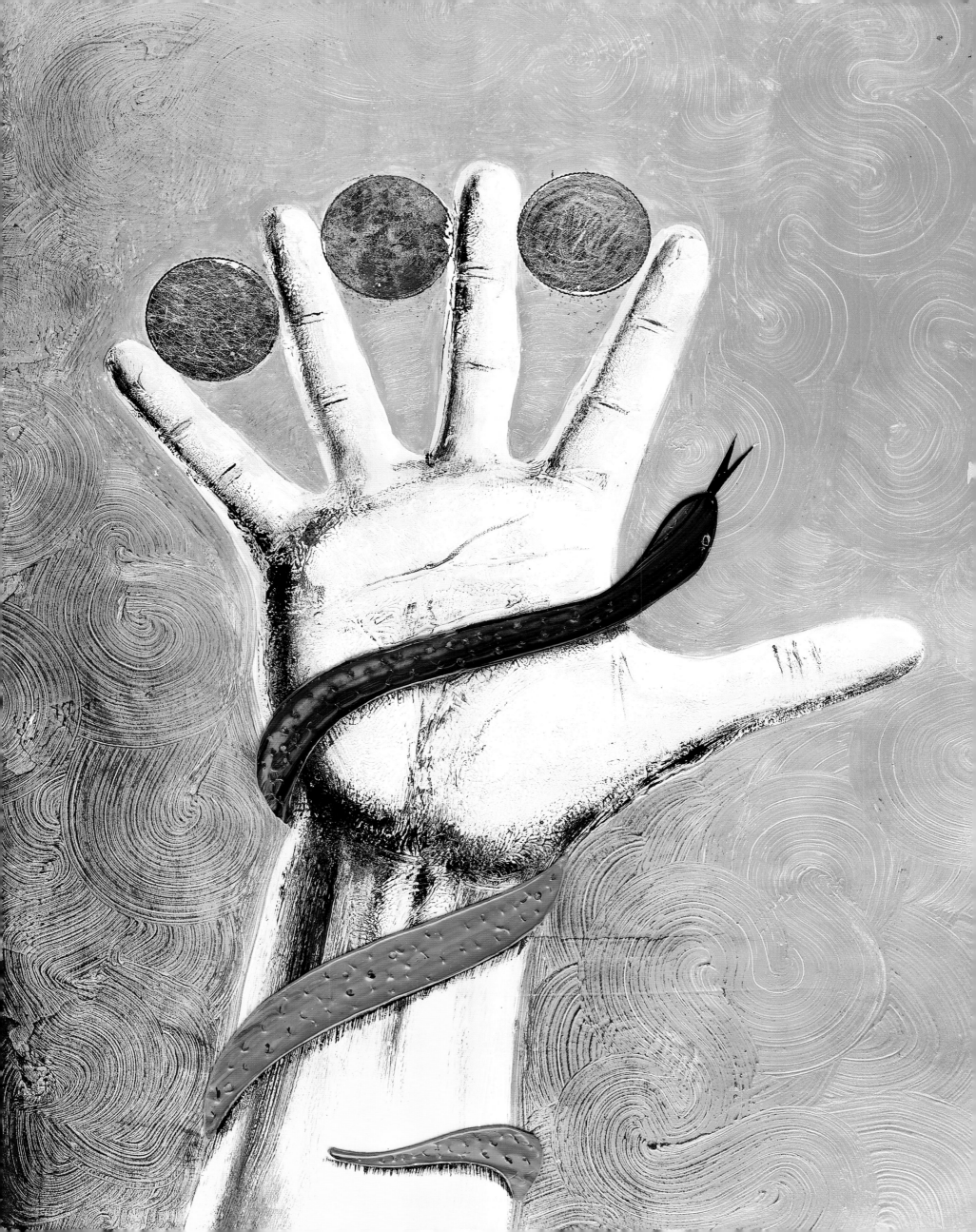

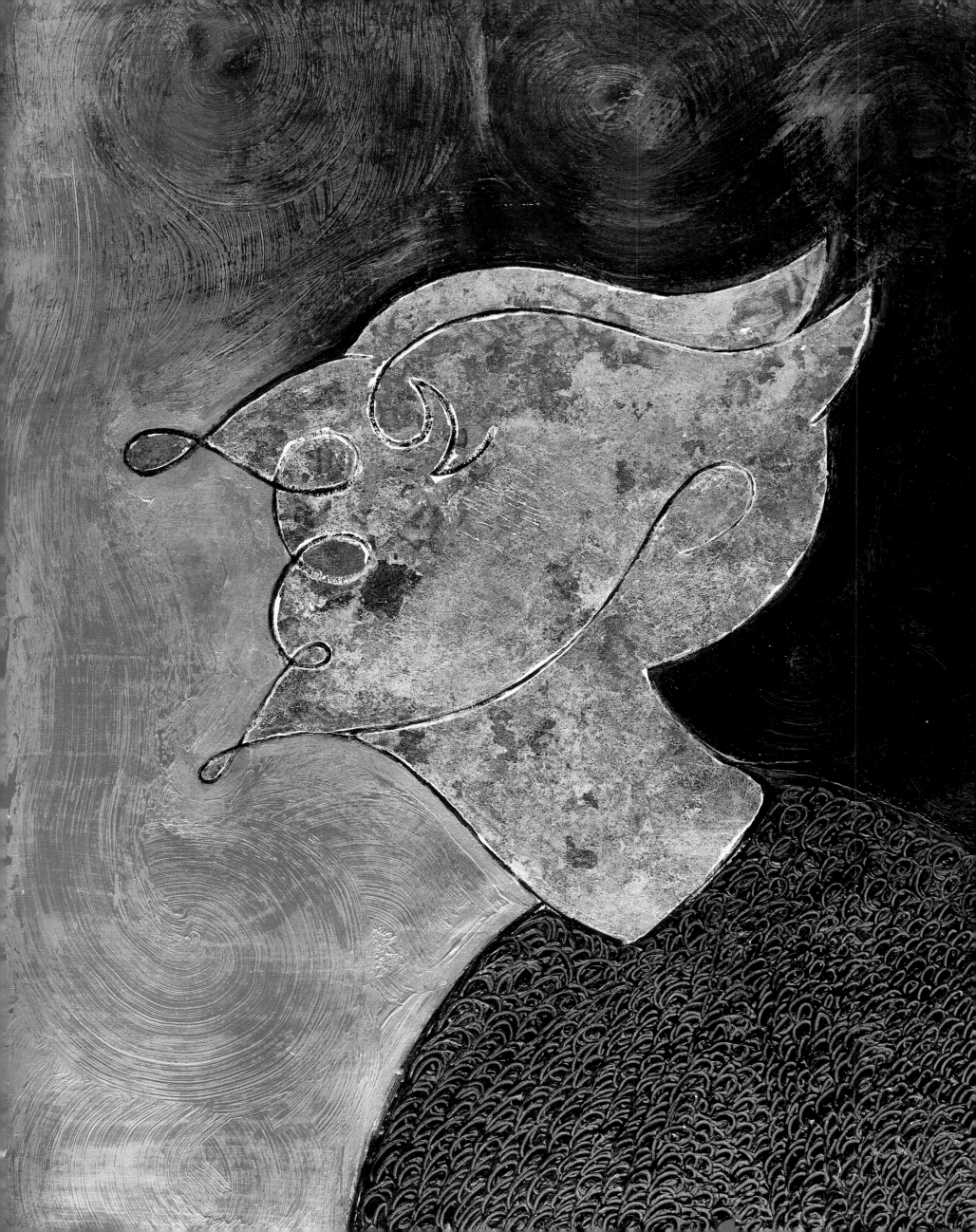

A miniature city had just been built. It was a big media event. Tom Brokaw was there for the opening broadcast. Nancy Ward was chosen as Queen of the city and she chose me as the King. I remember walking out on stage to stand next to Nancy. Sam and David were in the audience. Sam was laughing because she knew I didn't like all this kind of attention. Because we were King and Queen we had to be married. The wedding was about to begin, I looked to my left and saw a long line of people getting married or ready to be married in one big ceremony. Next to me was Steven Abrams and his wife. I made some comment and he said something about not punching me in the mouth. I think it was said in gest. I think the long line of people getting married were all people I knew from my past. I was having a very good time, Nancy was very funny as usual and I was disappointed when the alarm woke me.

I don't remember the begining of this dream but I was at Jay and Margo's house. It looked more like the appartment Jay and I had together when we were students at Art Center. I don't remember any furniture in the place. Jay and I were sitting on the dining room floor. We were talking when Jays older daughter came in the room. It was the first time we had ever seen each other. There was a moment I felt a little strange but it passed quickly when she hugged me. Then the other daughter came in, she was a little more shy but it was ok. Margo was in the living room. I get the impression she was ironing. Margo said something to the effect of I so glad were all back together again. Margo sat next to me, she put her hand on my back and rested her head on my shoulder.

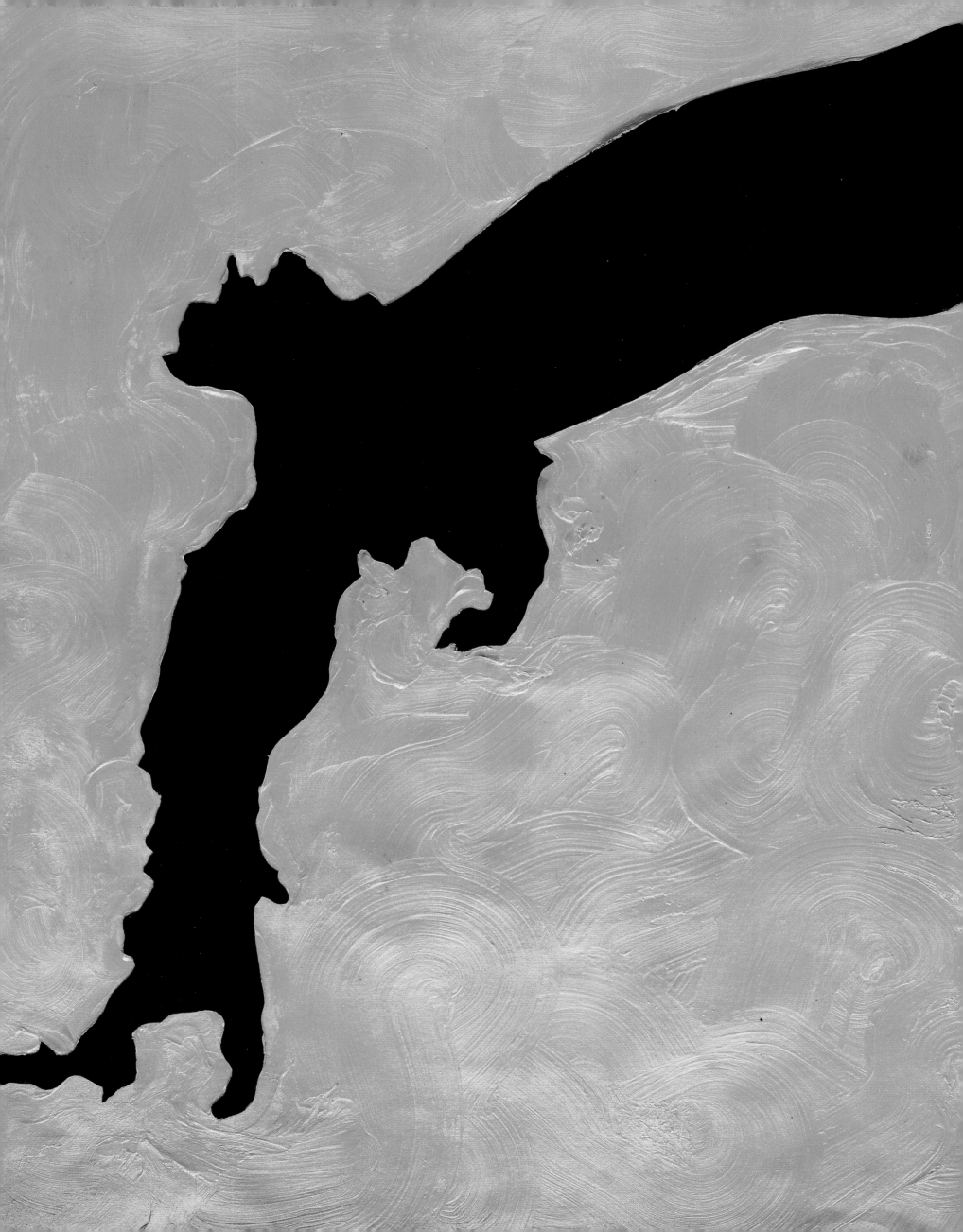

Ci Sono due gatti
con la terrazza
La mama e il
bambino
tutt'e due gatti
Sono timidi
Do cibo ogni
Mattina

HOTEL VILLA AURORA
★ ★ ★ ★

FIESOLE

June 1998

HOTEL
VILLA AURORA
★★★★
FIESOLE

I have had this dream before. There is a young boy. He is the only one who can see monsters others than me. They take many forms. Actual standard ugly monsters to shadows or feelings of something not quite right. I saw a white van pull out of a private driveway but the windows were opaque. At a public drinking fountain I saw a little plant like hand coming out of the drain. I cut it off with a knife then I stuck the knife down the drain I could feel something but could not see it. The boy and I try to tell others but no one will listen. I grabbed the boy's father (a military man) and tried to explain it is a matter of life and death. These dreams are always real heart pounders.

Albergo - Ristorante - Blu Bar - Meeting Place
Hotel Villa Aurora - Piazza Mino, 39 - 50014 Fiesole (Firenze) - Tel. 055/59.100 - 59.292 - Fax 59.587 - Teleg. Aurora Fiesole - Part. IVA 04455750481

I dreamed I went to the studio wearing only my underwear and shoes. I was at my drawing table. I looked down and I was very surprised to see I had no clothes on. As luck would have it there was a bathrobe in my office. I put it on and walked through the office. People were laughing. I was at talking with Dave and we agreed it was a very stressful time. ———————

I am in Fiesole. I take a taxi into Florence. I go to a cafe for lunch. In the cafe there are a small group of soldiers. One of the soldiers is a beautiful woman. She is saying something to me like she knows me. I go over to her table and sit next to her. We are talking I don't know what we are saying. Our heads are almost touching the table and our lips are almost touching.

I was looking for Jay. I was very angry at him. He had taken a photo from one of my Journals without asking me. I remember looking around a large house. I found a girl in what seemed to be a bed like you would find in a train. I finally found Jay. He was asleep in a big bed with curtains all around it he was rolled up in a blanket against the wall. Then we were sitting outside at a cafe like setting

I noticed one of the other soldiers looking at us, he seemed quite surprised to see us talking this way. Then we start start kissing and kissing more passionately I know there was more to this dream but this is all I can remember right now.

6/2/98

from Joyce T.

CONTINUE ON NEXT PAGE

venerdi pomeriggio

bottiglia

I said where is my photo!. He gave a poster to me of a French photographer, it was a black and white art poster and it was mine but it was not the photo I wanted. This time I pulled his hair and held it and demanded my Joyce Tenneson photo he took from my journal. Now the odd thing is, every time I pulled his hair, (which was several times during the course of our conversation) he was a young girl with long reddish hair, but he was still gay in voice and manner. Then he said "Oh I guess I should have told you ~~I~~ I gave it to the leader of some cult group for her to consider buying". I pulled his hair again and said how dare you try to make money from something of mine you

had nothing to do with. I demanded he return the photo. I don't remember how it was resolved and I think maybe the poster was taken (not sure) Then I was sitting in a cafe looking out of a round window. I saw a red Rolls Royce pull up in front of the window. The driver was Paul McCartney. He wore a red silk cape the was actually a pancho. I thought I should introduce myself by saying I was a good friend of Jenny Wallace but I was trying to think which ~~~~ name he knew her better by Boyd, Fleetwood or Wallace. This is where the dream ended.

6/3/98

Venerdi Pomeriggio

bottiglia tre

Boris Karloff ~~was~~ the incubus. I don't know if he was sick or dying or just old, but there was a real urgency to find or make a new incubus.

___

I found piles of dog shit in my backyard. I couldn't understand why Andy, our gardener had not cleaned up this mass of shit from Nell and Flossy.

___

I was hanging out with Jim Morrison of the Doors. I was driving us around San Francisco. We were both tripping on LSD. I remember going up and down the hills and ~~seeing~~ people in vivid colors and multiple images. Normally, if I were ~~awake~~ awake this would be my worst nightmare, but in this dream I was having a good time.

___

In 1984 I was living in London. Everyday I took the train from Chiswick to Covent Garden. One day as I boarded the train and took my seat I noticed an advertisement above the seat across the isle from me. The visual was a scene from Jack and the Beanstalk. I began to think of the story and remembered there was a chicken that laid golden eggs. I thought most people don't remember the chicken in this story. Then I began to ponder the meaning of golden eggs and then which naturally led me to the story of the goose that laid the golden egg. I pondered the meaning deeper really began to concentrate on golden eggs. As the train pulled into the next station a young man got on and sat down on the seat across from me. He was a nice looking young man maybe about twenty years old give or take a year or two. The train pulled out of the station and I noticed the young man reach into his pocket. To my surprise he took from his pocket a gold egg. He held the egg out as if showing the egg. Then he opened the egg to reveal another golden egg inside. He then closed the egg put it back in his pocket

and got off the train at the next station. Needless to say I was, as they say in England gob smacked. With 20/20 hind sight I wish I had spoken to the young man but I guess I was so surprised I didn't think to say anything. This was no dream and I can still see this event as clear as the day it happened, over fourteen years ago.

On one hand I don't want to over analyse what happened but on the other hand I have thought about this event many times over the last fourteen years and I wish I had a deeper understanding maybe if I paint the image a few times I can have a better relationship with the meaning of that encounter on the train.

For some reason I have had the occasion to tell this story several times in the last few weeks. For some reason the golden egg has been on my mind more than usual lately.

October 31, 1998

I was in a house at the beach. I was standing at a screen door looking out to a cove like area. looking through the screen I saw my old girl-friend Susie Durkee. She was sitting in the sand when her husband came up to her, he said something and they ran away together. I thought she still looked very pretty but also thought she had put on a little too much weight in her rear end. I went outside, as I walked to the shore line I saw a dead horse burried almost entirely in the sand. to the side of me down the beach a little ways was a crowd of people. I went over to see what was going on but by this time the crowd was gone. there was a teenage boy covering the skeleton of another horse with sand. The boy was deaf but knew when I was speaking to him. He said, "are you here for the coin?" I didn't know what he meant but realized the coin was a contribution to another boy. I was brushing the sand off of the horse skeleton and saw that all the bones had been beautifuly carved showing somekind of symbols. We talked about something to do with the other boy, (I wish I could remember what was said) This teenage boy seemed to have some mystic aura about him.

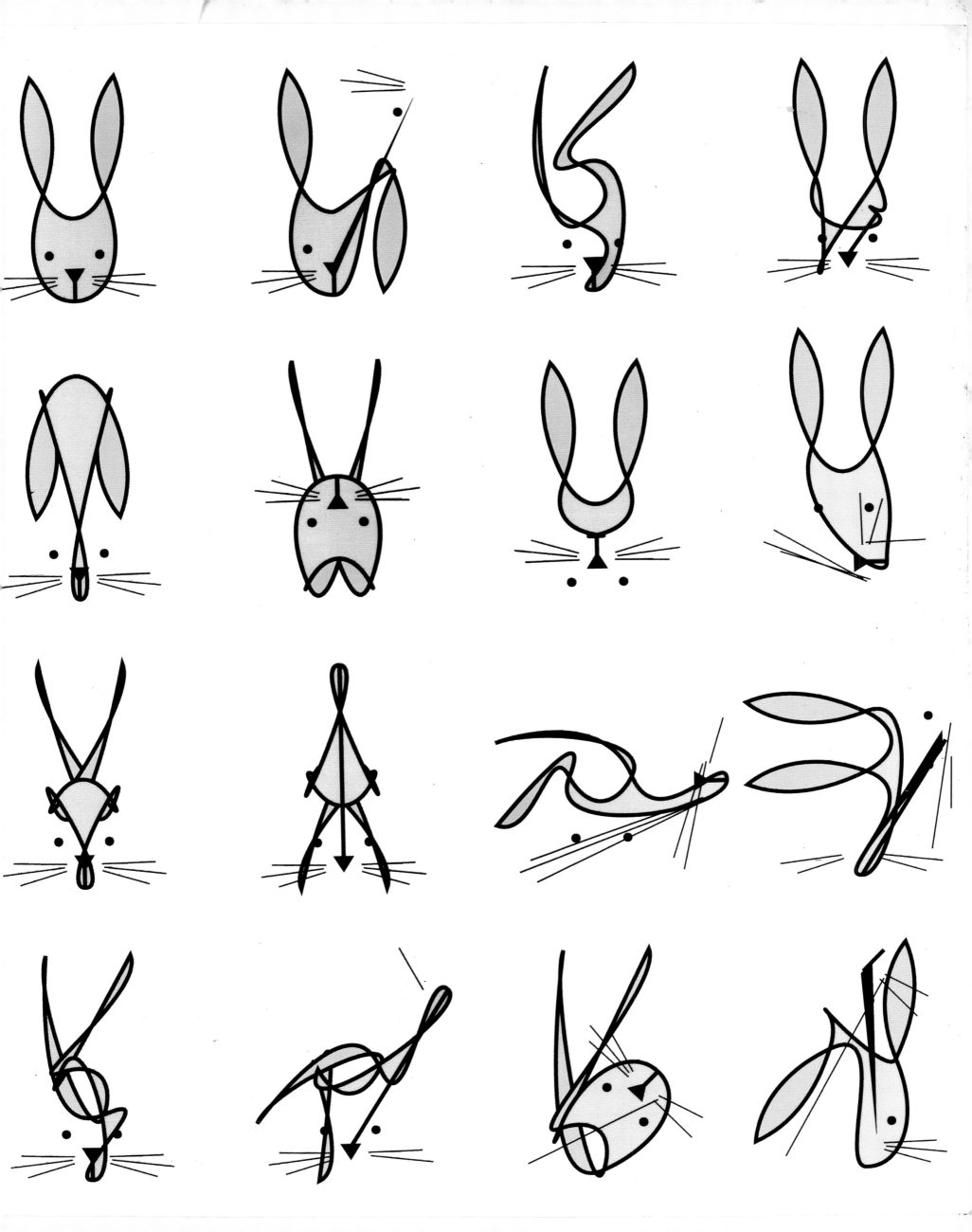

I had just finished a session with Marvin. We were walking through his garden. It was more like a desert garden, pretty but not a lush english type garden. We were walking and talking. then in a living room like room he said I should take three months off from our sessions. He was going to Europe and it made sense. I didn't mind the idea but I guess I had a surprised look on my face. He felt we should have one more session. He put his arm on my shoulders and said come on. I'll see you now. Marvin wanted to do this session in a movie theater. It was a wonderful old theater with wood paneled walls and nice detail like you don't see anymore. We went into a private room. In the room was a bed and a movie screen. Marvin went into what looked like a locker room bathroom kind of room. I sat on the bed. Marvin come out dressed in pajamas and got into bed. By now I was in bed too. When the movie started a voice said to get the best results from this movie it is recomended to hold hands. So here we are Marvin and I in bed holding hands watching this movie. It didn't feel gay or weird at all. The movie was a remake of an older film. The stars were from now and from a much earlier period of time.

The only actor I can remember is James Caan. Marvin said in this remake he lands in the middle of a basketball game. I was watching the movie a James Caan as a football play fell from the sky through the roof of the arena into the middle of a pro basketball game. All I can remember are the basketball players coming over to see this guy laying on the court. I know this movie was to have some message in it but what I don't know.

━━━━━━━━━━━━━━━━

I had just finished a game of tennis when I found myself at a mall or some kind of public place. Because of the tennis game an incision from a hemorrhoid procedure had opened up and was bleeding. I saw the blood on my hand and realized it was totally naked. I began to run, I think for my car and maybe some clothing.

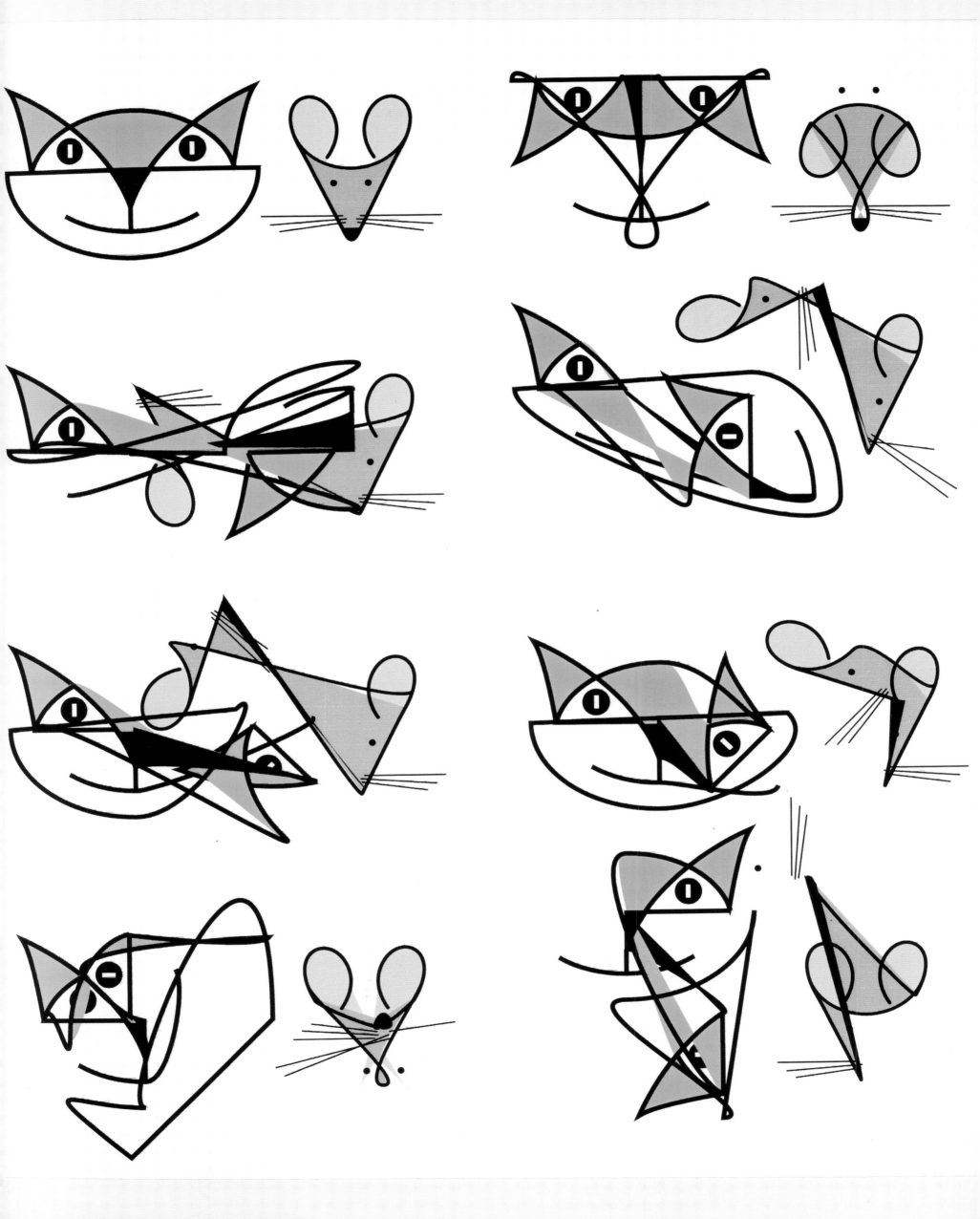

I was at Marvin office. It didn't look like Marvins office, it was more like a small ~~apartment~~ apartment, very average looking. I don't remember the conversation but I do remember Jay was there. I don't think it felt bad in any way. In fact I think it was a pleasant atmosphere. When the session was over I said I had to pee. Unlike Marvins real office I would have to walk through the living room into the next persons session When I went to the bathroom door it was divided into two halves, one above the other. The lower half was a very small door, maybe two feet high. As I was trying to enter the bathroom through the small door the next client of Marvins showed up. I could not fit through the small door. At the toilet I was having trouble peeing In my hand were a bunch of asperin I wanted to take three asperin but put the whole handful in my mouth When I did that I thought what am I doing and spit out the asperin. I thought I was spitting the asperin in the toilet but when I looked up I saw chewed asperin all over the wall. The bathroom door was ajar and I could see Marvins client waiting. I hadn't peed much and felt like I needed to pee more but I felt like I should get going

I wiped the asperin off the wall, there was alot of it but I noticed there was a lot of other stuff in the wall even chewing gum. There was a hair dryer hanging on the wall I think I was aware of a bathroom that was used by Marvin and his wife every day but thought there must be another more private bathroom connected to a master suite. I remember leaving the bathroom still feeling I needed to pee.

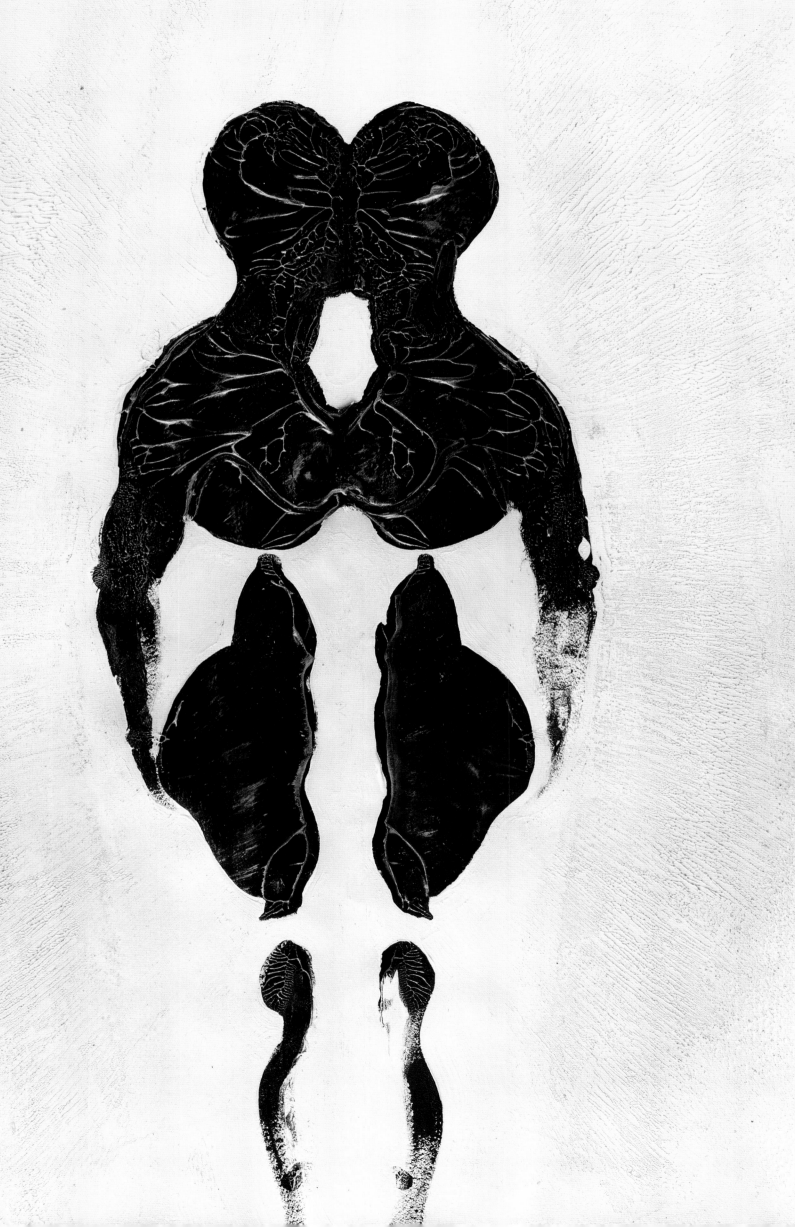

I entered a house, I think with Jay, Margo and Sandra. The house seemed to be a New York type house. It was big inside, kind of a dark ominous place. I don't remember a lot about the dream. I seem to remember walking around the place. The next thing I can recall is being in bed by myself. I was holding a trumpet mouth piece. When I looked through the large end I could see Jay in bed in another bedroom, I think the bedroom was on another floor. I also had the ability to scare Jay while I was looking through the mouth piece. Also it seemed I could see my father at the same time, sort of a split screen effect at the ~~too~~ end of the mouth piece tube. Then there seemed to be another entity in the house. It said the name Hillary Frontier. This ~~force~~ was very ~~scary~~ scarey and I ~~awoke~~ frightened, heart pounding from this dream.

I was with Sandra at the edge of a river. There was a house boat. The house boat was a wooden structure, kind of Tom Sawyerish. To get to the house boat you had to swim to it. Sandra was already on the houseboat. The river was very calm around ~~the~~ the houseboat, a bit turbulant in the middle and very rough further up river. I swam in the middle, I think it was the only way to get to the boat. I remember the water was brown from the churning of th river. When I got to the boat Sandra had a ~~stopwatch~~ stopwatch, she said that was X amount of minutes. I was surprised I had been swimming so long. We were in bed I had to pee. I was going outside to pee, I had to open a sliding door and a screen door. I was making noise and Sandra was mad.

I dreamed I was in bed with Farah Fawat. I don't know where we were but it seemed to be in medieval times for some reason. There was another man in the bed. We each were carressing a leg and kissing it. She was wearing paisley stockings. She said you can take off my stockings. As we both removed the stockings I was kissing her leg and when the stocking was off I smelled it. It had a fresh bath powder smell I thought it was very sexy. The other man was gone now. I was feeling her crotch I could feel her pubic hair. She said you can take off my underwear now. They were matching paisley print the same as her stockings. As I removed them I was kissing her ass there was that same bath powder smell and I smelled her underwear when I took them all the way off. I had a major hard on and wanted to fuck her right away but I didn't want to have this encounter end too soon. Then I was in a big official building. Where I had to go in the building seemed to be way in the back. There were two doors, one double one single. I don't remember which one I took but I found myself in a courtyard at Kathleens apartment. I went in and she said she had to tell me something but she wanted to tell me and Jay at the same time. I said fine but I have

to use the bathroom first. I stood at the toilet, there was a clothes rack next to the toilet. A couple of articles of clothing were ~~the~~ partly in the toilet. I put the wet clothing all the way back on the clothes rack and began to pee. I was still thinking about Farah. The entire dream seemed to be in a dark atmosphere, night time and dim lighting, dark rich colors. The official building seemed to belong to a famous shrink, Jung or freud or some famous shrink in general, its just a feeling I don't remember for sure.

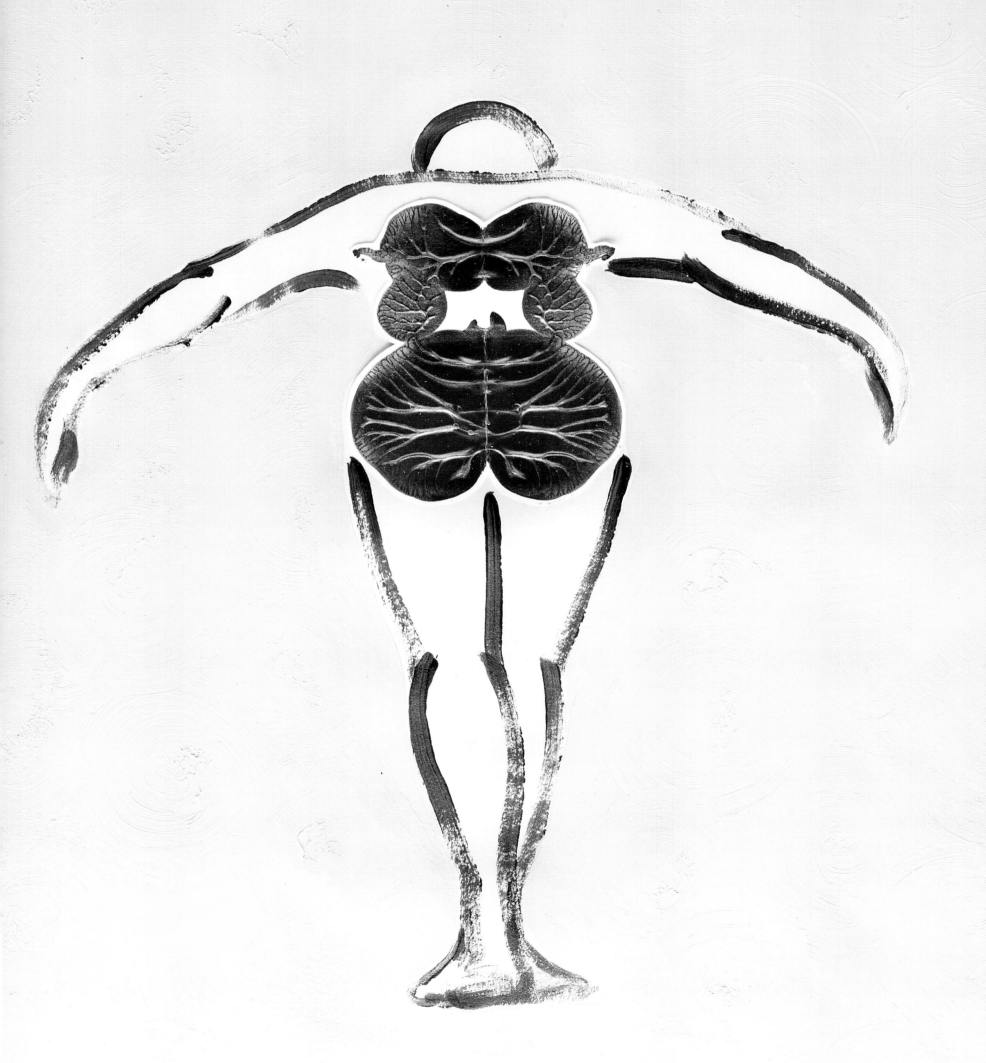

State Worker · Legally drunk · Exact estimate · Act naturally Found missing · Resident Alien · Genuine imitation Airline food · Good grief · Government organization Sanitary landfill · Alone together · Small crowd Business ethics · Soft rock · Butt head · Military intelligence · Sweet sorrow · Rural metro · Now then Passive aggression · clearly misunderstood · Peace force Extinct life · Plastic glasses · Terribly pleased · computer security · political science · Tight slacks Definite maybe · Pretty ugly · Rap music · working vacation · Religious tolerance · Microsoft works sweet and sour · Advanced basic · Same difference almost exactly · Silent scream · Living dead · Dry wine feeling numb · climb down · Black light · Bittersweet games · Awful pretty

Bad health · war unbiased opinion · Mighty weak · appropriate · past crystal · awful stop · Russian nickel · Virtual fits all · a little park · Home office · lawyer · Jumbo chile · Guest smaller · Fresh begun · Frozen annual · meat · more equal ·

thunderous silence a little big · oddly present · Liquid pretty · Rolling economy · wooden reality · One size pregnant · Industrial Hard water · Honest shrimp · Hot host · Crow frozen · finally burn · first less hamburger Moldy cheese Scottish Danish

**EMBASSY
SUITES**®

RESORT

Mandalay Beach

I was a chinese Kung Fu artist, but there seemed to be another Kung Fu artist who had some kind of power over me. He dominated me and even though I knew my strength or capability he went so far as to slap me across the face. He seemed to be going somewhere but did not ~~want~~ wish to take me. I demonstrated my great skill by doing a beautiful Kung Fu routine and he had to change his attitude about me.

Sandra was having a baby in six weeks and I was freaked out. I could not imagine giving up my life as I know it for so many years. Was it going to be a ~~boy~~ or a girl? How would I relate to it? How much sleep would I loose. I had my head in my hands crying from the thought of it and all around everyone was just fine. Mom was living with us. I said because this is a two bedroom house it would be easier for you to find an apartment than for me to buy a new house. She agreed without hesitation.

Sandra and I were sitting on a beach. We were both masterbating. When we had finished George Harrison walked by in back of Sandra and dropped a dark colored seed in her lap. For some reason she took this as some kind of insult and got up to go over to him and let him know she was angry. He was standing in the water talking to someone. The next thing I remember is finding Sandra apparently dead. George Harrison had tied her to something and she had spent the night under water, it's not clear but he had tried to kill her. I was crying, the loss felt too much to bare. I picked her up and started to search for a hospital. When I finally did find one it was a Childs hospital. Jeff Duvas was the doctor. He said Sandra had a 50/50 chance to live ~~t~~ but even if she did live she could have brain damage that could effect her career as a shrink. Then I went to my friend David Love ~~~~ at his office in London. I asked if we could use a private office to talk. In the office I told David what had happened. I was very distraught and he was very understanding.

1-13-01 L.A.

Mom had died. Jay, Margo, Sandra and I were sitting at a table sorting through her things, boxes or containers looking for gold. At one point I found something that looked like gold. It was only a small gold leaf like piece. Then I remembered a conversation I had had with mom about some pouch like things where she would keep valuable things. Sitting at the table I saw these pouches. Inside one of them was an assortment of gold rings. I think I said AHA! and began to put the rings in my pocket. Jay got angry that I was taking all the gold for myself. He got up from the table and began to grab at me and my pocket. I said OK thats it, lets have it out right now. We began to fight, I knew I would beat the shit out of him. I thought maybe I should take off my shirt so he could see my muscles and that that would scare him. The fight woke me up, my heart was really pounding.

April 8, 01 L.A.

I heard that my mother had cancer. It seems as if we were living together in a two-story house, me my mom and Sandra. My mother went down stairs to visit with some of her friends. I could hear them talking. I don't know exactly what they were saying but I think they were trying to cheer her up and they were giving her presents. She came upstairs, she was in bed. I came in the room to talk to her and see if she was alright or if she wanted anything. I think I asked her to show me what her friends had given her or I wanted to show her something but she was too tired. I left the room and turned out the lights in the hallway but when ever I turned out a light another light went on. This was a square shaped area in the upstairs hall or sort of a landing. I was unable to turn off the lights.

The room was dark, someone came in I was afraid Jay was so angry he might try to hurt me while I slept. The person sat on the bed, I said is that you Amber? Sandra replied no, its me I was relieved and glad to wake up and be at home.

April 12, 01 L.A.

I was with Carole King and Lorna Guess and Jay. We were in an underground parking structure. For some reason I had been given a police car to drive around in. I put something in the trunk, I don't remember what it was but I had trouble gitting the trunk to stay closed. Eventually it did close and we started to drive out of the parking structure. There was a long line of cars waiting to leave but I thought as long as I had a police I could just go around everyone, so I did. I pulled out and turned left onto Sunset Blvd. heading towards B.H. I was driving fast, taking advantage of having the police car. There was a tree branch blocking both east bound lanes. I stopped the car, got out but now I had not been driving, I had been flying. I was flying high, only about six inches off the ground. I was wearing a cashmere shirt and I didn't want to ruin it while flying so close to the ground. I took the shirt off I noted perspiration stains under the arms. Jay was whining about something so I removed a baseball cap from my head and slapped him across the face very hard. Then I went to the trunk of the police car and took out a piece of carpet about 3' by 2' and we all took off flying up Sunset B still only about 6" off the ground. We arrived at home, Carole said just she had promised almost as if she had been piloting the carpet. I found it curious. At home I was in bed was thinking I had been very mean to Jay and I should say I'm sorry

Aug. 6, 01 L. A.

I was at the beach with Bob and Ron. It was a foggy morning, the sun was trying to burn through and we just finishing getting into our swim suits. I looked out at the waves and saw what I thought was smoke. I said look at that, there must be a boat on fire. Then I saw it was actually a spray of sand and water caused by hundreds of dolphins leaping straight up out of the water and everywhere they jumped up and landed it was like an explosion. As a result of each explosion hundreds of fish would fly up out of the water. I thought this was a way for the dolphins to catch food. There was one dolphin laying on the sand, it seemed to be hurt and there were people gathering around it. The atmosphere was eerie. I thought I saw a giant wave about to break close to shore but it turned out to be a trick of the light through the fog.

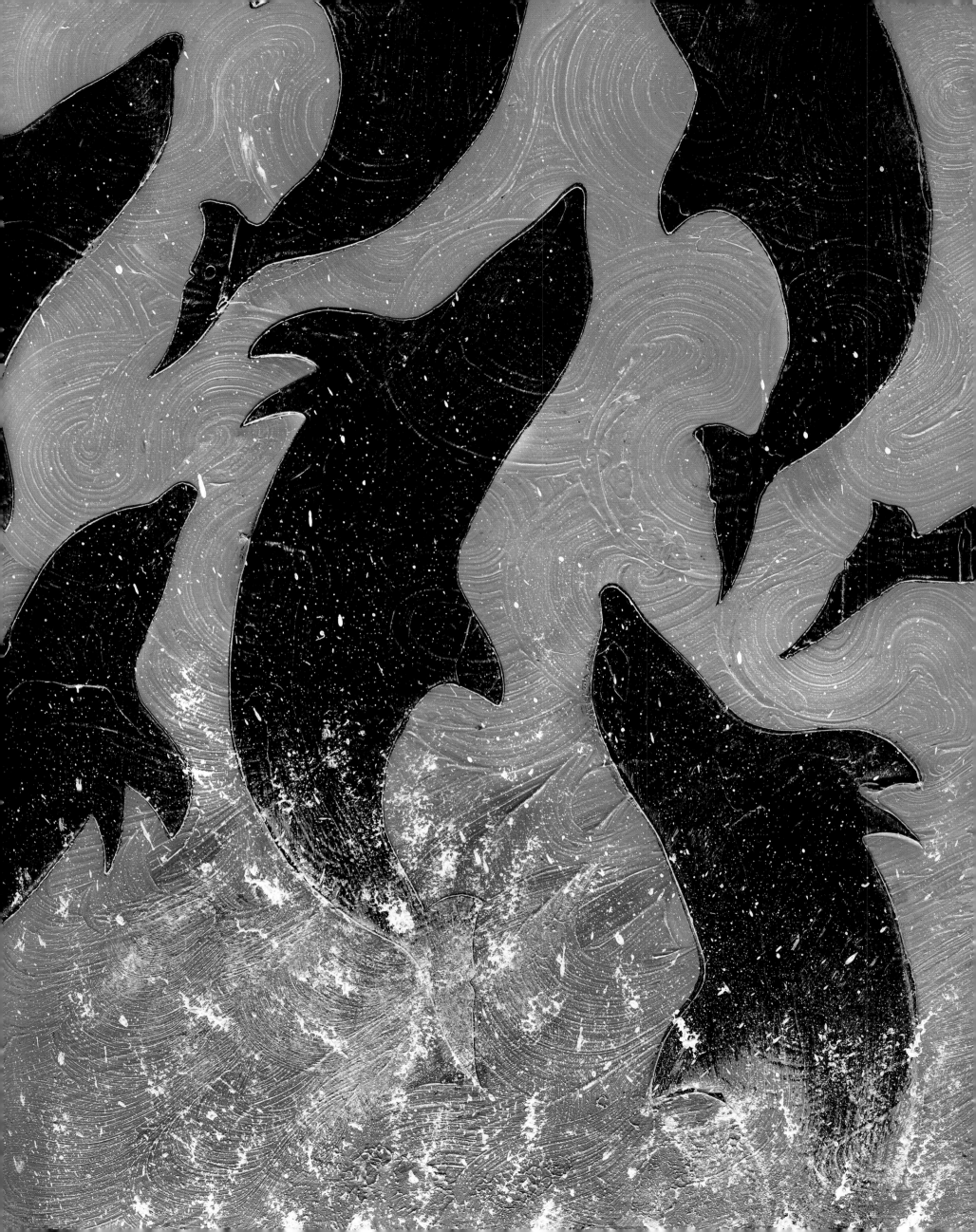

Oct. 27, 01 L.A.

Sandra and I were sitting in our living room.
Morgan and Jordan were there. They were now
coming over to our house and staying the weekend.
It felt very natural to have them there. Then
Sandra said where's Nell? I said Sandra
Nell is dead but why don't we get a new dog,
right now, today. Sandra said thats a very big
move how does it feel to you psychologically
speaking. I was sitting of the sofa in my bathrobe
and said I'm so tired, its Sunday as I laid down
I said I don't want to think about it.

Nov. 1, 01 L.A.

I was sleeping over a Jay and Margos place.
Jordan and I were sharing a room. Jordan and
I each had a twin bed. I was aware of the
fact the Jordan had disapproved of Morgans
meetings with me, so we wern't talking and I
was sleeping with my back towards her. Then
I ~~woke~~ woke up a 5AM to some 1970's rock &
roll. I went into Jay and Margos room and said,
whats going on, its 5AM? Margo was sitting at a
drawing board working on an illustration.
Jay was up and about he said something to the
effect of, its good to be up early and get started
on the days work. Then I went back into my room,
The Jordan that works for me was sitting on the
end of my bed working on ~~the~~ his computer.

Nov. 2, 01 L.A.

all I can remember are two dogs.

December 5, 01 L.A.

David told me that I should see a certian film. I rented the film and I guess I watched it on T.V. There was a man, I have no feel for what he was like or doing. There were a series of words appearing on screen As the movie went on the words seemed to became fewer and fewer as if leading up to one last word. Also at the same time there was a ball forming. I can't remember how it was forming, maybe pulling from everything around it. It was a smooth light gray ball about the size of a basketball when it had reached full size. Then one last word appeared on screen and I was seeing the earth from space. Then there was a huge Atomic explosion. The explosion was so big it knocked the earth off of its axis. The earth went spinning out of control and began crashing into the other planets and eventually destroyed the entire solar system. Then I thought what about all of the souls that were somehow attached to earth or what would happen to souls that were to be reincarnated, where would they go? Or did it matter at all to these souls, were they on a deferent plane we don't have any concept of. These souls were already existing in space and that the earth wasn't really neccesary in the grand scheme of things. These souls would travel on to other universes or solar systems. I wish I could remember that word.

Dec. 26, 01 L.A.

I was in a Mexican barrio, sitting on a step on the street. I was sitting with Michel Richards and I think Art Snyder. The reason I was there with Michael was that we were working on a project together. I asked him a question and he said he had not done the research, I said, thats ok I already found my inspiration. Michel gave me a friendly elbow in the side and said something to the effect of "excuse me". We were watching people go by and then Michel pulled a diamond bracelet out of my pants pocket. I said something like, oh I must remember to do something with that or give it to Sandra and I put it back in my other pocket. Then two Mexican guys walked by with a baby girl. One of the guys did not have a shirt on. The baby wore a white sheet in a toga like fashion and a black top hat, kind of like a New Years baby. The baby walked over to us and the shirtless guy came over and picked her up. As he picked her up he said something to Michel in Spanish but what I heard sounded just like Italian. I said I know what he said, (studiamo molto) we study alot. Now Michel was Raul Vega. Raul said, no it is part of a story. As we walked away in different directions I was sure I had it right.

Feb. 11, 02 L.A.

I was in a room with
Sandra and one other person
that doesn't figure into the
dream. A gay friend of ours
entered the room, he was
elated because he had
just heard he was going to
be a grandfather. I was
watching Sandra's face,
I couldn't figure out how
she was reacting to the news.
She had kind of a funny look
on her face but then she got
up & very eagerly congradu-
ated our friend. Then our friend
told us more detail about the up
coming birth. It turns out that
the father of the baby is Eric
Clapton. Also our friend is worried
because the Woman giving birth is
going to do an out of the hospital
birth that is a little ~~~~ unusal.
The method of birth is to lay on a raft
made of rubber. The raft is in a very slow
moving river next to the shore. The womans
hands are tied over her head to the top of
the raft, so she is unable to use her arms or
hands. We are now watching a home movie
of this type of birth. There is a woman tied to
a raft and a couple of people helping her. Then
the camera pans the scene after the birth,
we see a lot of blood on the raft and in the
water but we also feel it is natural to see
this amount of blood with child birth.

Feb. 15, 02 L.A.

Brian and I were walking through a canyon. The first part of the trip was on dry land. Then we came to a large area I had seen before. Usually this area had a small water hole, the size of a normal swimming pool, but now because it had rained a lot (I thought) the entire area was filled. It had now become a giant lake. The water in this lake was the most beautiful blue water I had ever seen. Brian and I each had swimming pool rafts and we set out to cross the lake. As we were floating across the lake and I was looking at the water I said to Brian "hey Brian look, this water is effervescent!" You could see the surface of the water fizzing like a ~~it~~ freshly poured carbonated drink. When we reached the shore we had to go under water to go through an opening in the rocks. Brian and I pushed our rafts through the opening and swam through. We came out in a grotto like place open at both ends, some water and some dry areas. Brian found a bag of camera equipment it seemed to be his and he was busy going through it. I dove back down in the water to see if we could get back. For some reason it was impossible to go back through the hole and some other passages were blocked with ~~to~~ chain link fencing, we could not go back. I looked ahead of us, the canyon narrowed again but it was filled with the beautiful blue effervescent water, the sun was shining and going forward was a good thing.

Feb. 26, 02 L.A.

I was walking in a neighborhood. It was an uphill walk on a street lined with nice houses. I had never seen this area before but I seemed to know where I was going. I was going to the top of the street to see a fountain and a natural waterfall. When I reached the fountain at the top of the street I saw two people sleeping in sleeping bags on cots, one of them was Sam. I thought it was quite cold to be sleeping outside. I went up past the ~~water fall towards the~~ fountain towards the waterfall and there was Flossie. She was so glad to see me, she was young and healthy and would not stop licking me.

Feb. 26, 02 L.A.

I was in Florence in a time before cars. There were carriages and horses and lots of people walking. I rode in a carriage with Spencer Tracy. Jay and Margo were there and I talked with a beautiful black girl that was an art model.

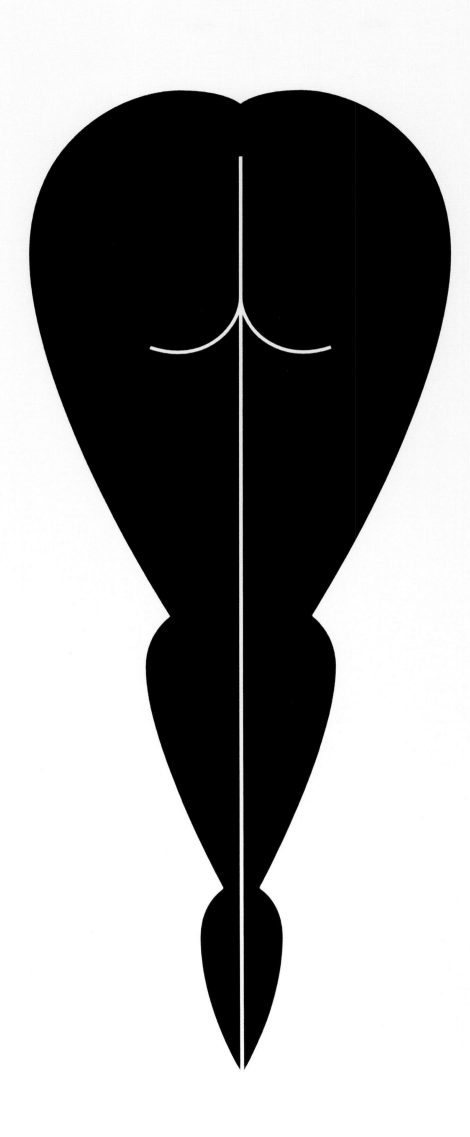

March 1, 02 L. A.

I was going to be in a movie. The movie was being produced by or directed by John McVie. My part in the film along with Jayme Odgers was to be dressed like Indian women. There was a meeting with McVie, we laughed about something and he patted me on the back as I was leaving for the evening. I was in a parking lot, going to my new Fiat sports car when I ran into Jay. I greeted him in a very friendly manner and we went to have a drink. I told Jay I had a part in this new film. He seemed upset about me being an actor. He said that was something he should be doing, that it was something he had always wanted to do. Then he became more angry and said, don't you know how successful I am, where I am in my career, I'm at the top, everyone thinks I'm great. Jay's bragging didn't really bother me and I left to find my car. When I got out to the parking lot I discovered my new car had been stolen.

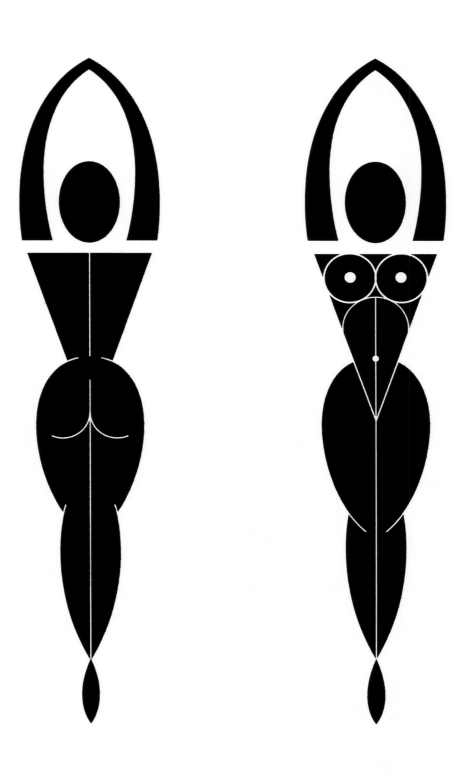

March 17, 02 L.A.

I was standing outside my office. I was with Dave and one or two other people. I was looking at the hills in the direction of my house. I saw a large column of smoke rising from the Nichols Canyon area and I started running towards home. Dave and the other people also ran with me. For some reason even with a emergency at home I felt it necessary to show everyone that I could run faster than they could. As I ran at this fast pace I could not run in a straight line, I kept veering to the right, it was out of my control. I think I even hit a rock wall. On the way to my house I stopped at the house of Barbra and Hilton. I ran in without knocking and I yelled for Barbara. Barbara and Hilton both said "were here but don't come in the bedroom." It was obvious when Barbara came to the door of the bedroom with a sheet around her and one breast exposed that I had interrupted them in the middle of sex. I warned them of the fire and ran to my house. My mother was living with us and as I entered the house I yelled for her. I told her of it danger of the fire but she seemed not to be too worried. I made her come outside on the patio to see just how bad the situation was. There was fire everywhere. you could see it jump from tree to tree and house to house but she still was not concerned. When it was all over our house was the only one left standing. The whole canyon was black and smoking. I thought I must photograph this scene.

April 16, 02 L.A.

Sandra and I were out with the cast of Seinfeld. I don't know where we went, a restaurant I think. On the way back we were all in the same car. It was a small car so we were all scrunched together. Jerry was driving, I was in the front and so was one of the others. Sandra was in the back with the rest of the cast. We were driving through an L.A. canyon, we came to a house that was under construction. There was a passage through the center of the house. Jerry drove through the passage way, and out to the canyon road. The home was hughe. It turned out that the home was Jerry's new home. Then I had a wad of toilet paper in my hand. I was wiping my ass and worried that the others would notice. Then we arrived at Jerry's rented house. Sandra and I were going to spend the night at Jerry's place. Our room was not very nice at all. It seemed to be a guest room that had not been cleaned after the last guests had left. The room was not at all what we had expected.

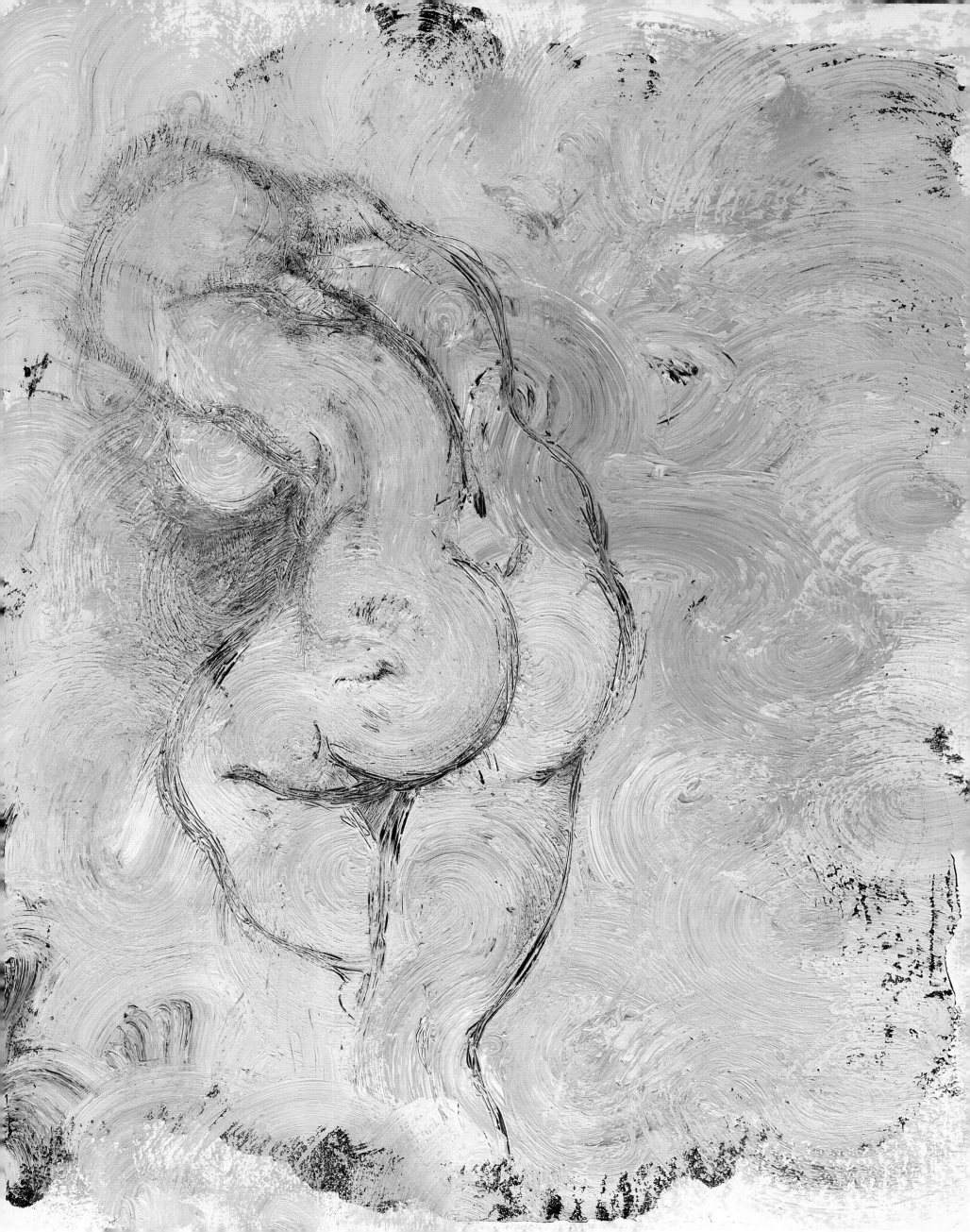

April 17, 02 L.A.

I was sharing a house with Marvin and his wife. The house was actually a houseboat. I remember looking around for the first time with Marvin, thinking there should be more of a view. Then Marvin showed me a beautiful sun room. I remember standing at the shore with Marvin talking about something but I don't remember what. I remember talking to Marvins daughter, an attractive young woman. We were in the sun room and I was reminiscing about the first time I had ever seen the sun room, it seemed like years ago.

Then Mike and Ann Peters came by the house boat for a visit. I met them on the dock. For some reason they walked up and down some stairs that were the long way around. We went inside the houseboat that was now a hotel. I wanted to get a table for three outside on the deck but it was a Saturday and very busy. I told the hostess (an older woman) that I was a resident on the boat but she said she couldn't help too much but she would try, but I should be prepared to wait.

April 27, 02 L.A.

I was on our patio lying on the ground next to the bird feeder. Two large birds landed on a branch above me. They were so bright red that at first I thought they were cardinals, but as they moved I could see that they were pidgons and it was the evening sun reflecting on the birds that caused them to appear to be red. Then as they turned they changed from light brown to bright pink. Then I heard a seagull. I thought it would be a good idea to move before the pidgons shit on me so I went to see what the seagull was doing making so much ~~noise~~ noise. The gull under the bird feeder with it head down a hole determined to catch a gopher. I slapped the gull on its back side and it made a WAAAA sound like a baby crying. I looked into the hole and out popped a gopher, it was very cute. I thought I might touch it, but considered the fact that it my bite me, so I decided not to touch the gopher. I woke up because I heard someone calling my name - But when I was totally awake I realized that it was actually a dog, half barking and half howling.

June 13, 02 L. A.

Sandra and I were at the beach. It was
still dark outside, just before dawn. There was
a beautiful light on the ocean and the quality
of the waves were most interesting. A pair of
ducks landed on the water near the shore. I
said to Sandra, I wish I had some food for
them. Then I saw half of a muffin laying in
the sand. I picked up the muffin, walked to
the edge of the water and began to feed the ducks.
Then the ocean parted near the shore and a woman
seemed to emerge from the waves. She looked like
a gypsy, dark hair lots of jewlery and a scarf
around her head. She said to me "You must Begin
to ride the Gods of the hand, in London". I said
WHAT? and she looked at me as if to say, hey I'm
giving you great words of wisdom here, but the look
was in jest and she was really caring. Then she
said again "Begin to ride the Gods of the hand in
London". Then the ocean closed and she melted
back into the waves.

Begin to Ride the Gods of the Hand in London.

June 15, 02 L.A.

Tom Cruse and I were driving down a coast highway. I was the driver and Tom was in the passenger seat. The waves that day really breaking well and there were a lot of surfers in the water. I saw one surfer getting a particulary good ride and asked Tom if he had ever tried to surf. He said yes, once, but he had wiped out. I told him I had surfed for many years. We arrived at a funky beach restaurant. There was live music and lots of people eating. As we walked by the restaurant to the beach you could hear people whispering "Tom Cruse just walked by". I wanted to ask him what it was like for him to hear that where ever he went that the dream seemed to end at that point.

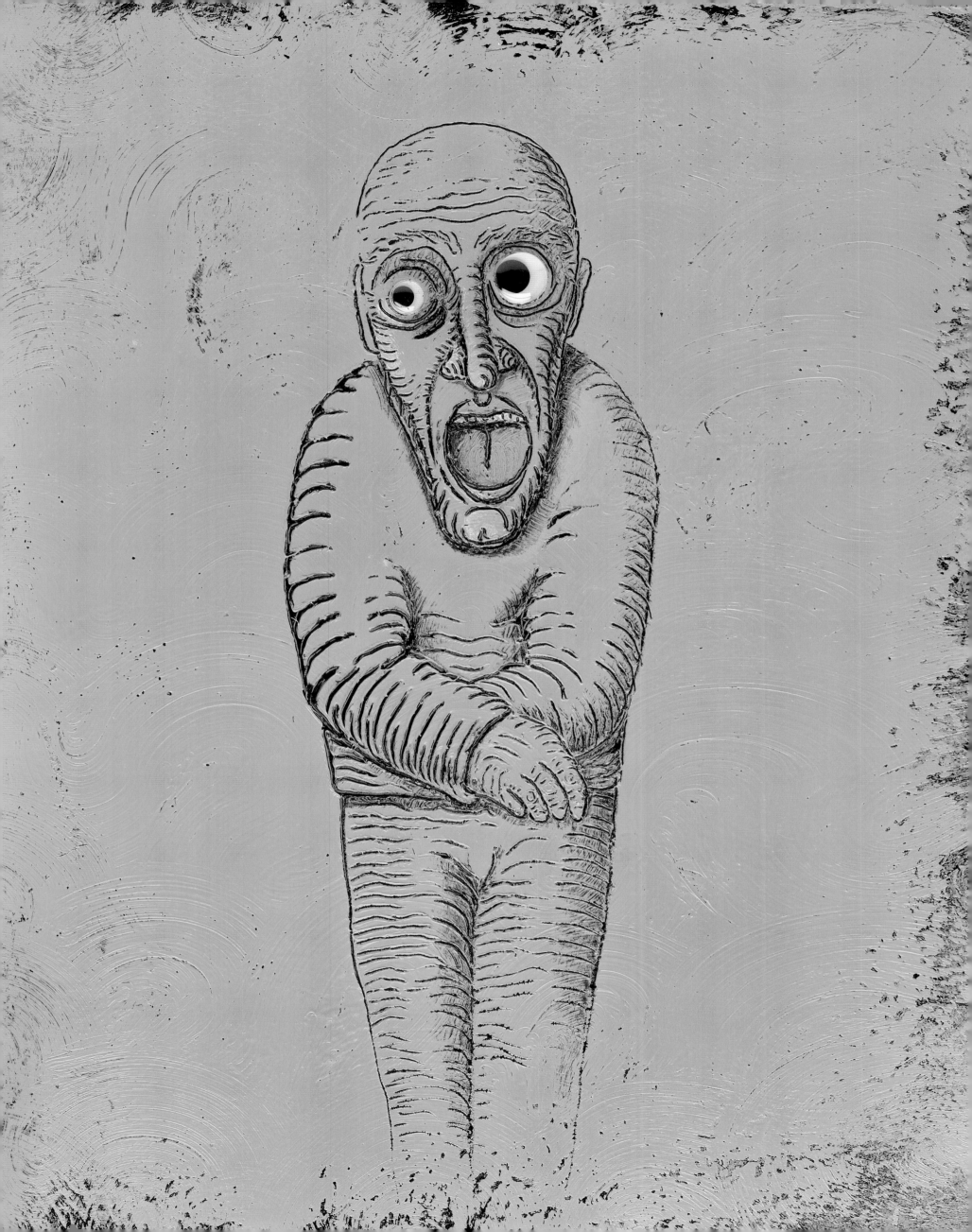

Sept. 24, 02 Ravello, Italy

I was with Mick Fleetwood, we went into a ~~motel~~ motel together. Lindsey Buckingham was there. Lindsey and I began to talk and ~~the~~ catch up on what we had been doing for the past few years. Lindsey said he was ~~now~~ a father of six. I was very surprised to hear he had decided to have such a big family. Then Lindsey told me he had a new guitar that had a very different sound and would I like to hear it. I said yes, and we went to another room in the motel. This room was large and it seemed Fleetwood Mac was recording a new album in this room. I saw Lindsey's new guitar and heard the great new sound. Then people started coming in, people I knew and a lot of new hanger-on types. Richard Dashut, Mickey Shapiro's ex partner Steve Steinberg and others. Christine McVie was there, dressed and acting more like Dame Edna and when she saw me she made a big fuss. She lavished me with hugs and kisses and then said to me, I'm glad that you are finally professionally slender. I didn't know what to make of the comment but took it as a compliment. I saw Judy Wong and tried to say hello to her but she either didn't hear me or didn't want to talk to me. I sat down next to her and attempted to make conversation but she didn't want anything to do with me. I was introduced to some of the new, younger people hanging around the band but they were not interested and had no idea who I was or my history with Fleetwood Mac.

Oct. 5, 02 Ravello, Italy

Sandra and I went to an amusement park with Brenda, Jake and Kizzy. We were seated outside to watch a movie. Sandra and I went into a theatre because we saw a poster for an act that was very ~~unus~~ unusual. It was a woman that could talk by farting. We thought we can't miss this. As we entered the theatre a woman that worked there came over to us. We said it was a shame that the theatre was being torn down for a development and that this was the last night. Then the woman said during the show the farting woman must leave the stage several times to have a shit. In the theatre we sat with Christine McVie. Christine saw John Hurt and introduced us. John and Sandra got on very well and she told him about the connection we already had at the Soho House in London. He laughed and remembered Norman's comment. John Hurt took a seat on the balcony. Mick Fleetwood came in and sat next to me. He was very pleased to see me and put his arm around me as we talked. Then Mick saw

John Hurt and because he knew him Mick went up to the balcony to say hello. When Mick reached John Hurt, John did a stunt fall to the floor and acted (very well) as if he was dying. Now for ~~some~~ some reason I had to leave the theatre. On the way out I saw the farting lady getting ready to go on stage. She was very pretty and looked right out of the 1920's. She was wearing a very sexy negligee with her bottom exposed. I then took a orange traffic cone, put it on its side and be-gan ~~to~~ to ride it like a skateboard through the amuse-ment park and the large parking lot. I was really good at this traffic cone riding. I arrived at an enterance to a building. I think there was valet parking and I can't remember the rest of the dream. ———

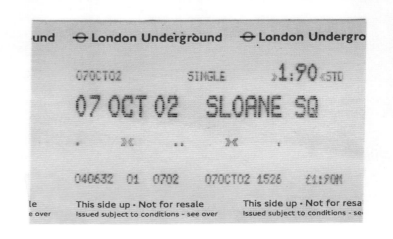

Oct. 30, 02 L.A.

Sandra and I were attending some kind of school. It seemed we were older than anyone else at the school. One day a group of boys that we were friendly with told us we had better leave the school at once because they had a bomb and they were going to set it off right away. Sandra and I left the school and for some reason we didn't warn anyone. ~~instead~~ instead we went to a place where there were a number of shops. I bought a Jesus made of bird seed. We heard the explosion and returned to th school after everyone was gone. There was just Sandra and I and a few of the boy that had set off the bomb. I think some teachers were killed and I don't know about th students. We walked around th first floor and the damage was not so bad. Then we went upstairs. The stairs were very badly damaged but we went up anyway.

The place looked exactly like our old apartment on Sycamore. We walked up the badly damaged back stairs and looked in all of the rooms starting in front and working our way back. The upstairs was heavily damaged. I don't remember anything ~~els~~ else that happened after that. ————————

Nov. 9, 02 L.A.

I went to see Bob Carbone. Bob was a dentist. I was sitting in a chair, Bob was going to do some kind of dental work on me but I don't know what it was. I was looking in a mirror so I could see what was going on inside my mouth. I said to Bob, don't you have to do a root canal as part of this procedure? He said yes as he pulled a string like thing from a lower tooth, it was the root he had just removed. It didn't ~~hurt~~ hurt at all. He said now a days it doesn't hurt anymore. I thanked him for his skill. He seemed even taller than usual. → skillful work.

November 12, 02 L.A.

My mom and I were going to go on a vacation together. Mom was talking about Alabama and Utah. I didn't like these choices so I went out on my own to find something more interesting. I found myself at the sea shore at a beautiful spot. The place was very rocky. There were hundreds of birds sitting on the rocks. There was a very large cave entrance with book shelves carved into the rock, giant book shelves with huge books sitting in the shelves. I thought the books would be ruined in the elements but then again the books had been there a long time and still looked good. Once inside the cave I saw crypts set into the cave walls. Raquel Welch was there looking for the crypt of an actor she had once worked with. She saw me and asked me to help her with something. I told her we had actually met once before at a party. At first I thought it was a party at Christine McVie's house but then I remembered it was Michael's Richards house. We had an emediate romantic attraction for eachother. There was a lot of hugging and kissing going on, then I said I needed to go to the bathroom. Then I was in Christine McVie's house. The house was huge and not at all like her actual home. The bathroom was downstairs but it was more like a public bathroom with multiple toilet stalls and a row of sinks. I went into one of the stalls and sat down to take a shit, but as soon as I sat down I noticed a large hole in the stall wall. I moved to the next stall just as Michael Richards entered the bathroom. He saw me going from one stall to the other and as he was leaving he said, don't worry I won't say anything I do some silly things myself.

Dec. 2, 02 L.A.

There was a Russian beauty queen that never thought she was very pretty. When ever she looked in the mirror she saw only imperfection. So the beauty queen hired someone to rip her eyes out. Now the Russian people didn't want her to represent their country any more because she was no longer pretty.

Dec. 3, 02 L.A.

All of the people in the world began to secrete a substance that looked like motor oil. The substance came from pores and seemed to seep and squirt from their bodies. I was the only one not suffering from this horrible affliction. This substance also came from animals, plants and even inanimate objects. It seemed to be the end of life as we know it. We had fucked up so bad that it was time to start over again.

Dec. 3, 02 L.A.

I was walking in a large indoor mall when I heard someone call my name. I looked around and saw three friends of mine. There was Shaquille O'Neal, a guy named Eddie a blind contestant on Jeopardy and one other guy. We talked for a while, Eddie said he hadn't run into me at the gym for a couple of weeks. Shaquille seemed to be part of my dreams for the rest of the night.

Dec. 29, 02   Santa Barbara (The White House)

I was at the beach with my father. My
father had with him a dog. The dog was black
and seemed to be a friendly well adjusted dog
as it played in the surf. When the dog came out
of the water I could see what looked to be a
large boil like thing on one of its hind legs, on
the hip area. Then I noticed that there was a lot
of hair missing from its back and side. Not an
animal you would want to get close to, to pet or
snuggle. Then the dog was led away on a leash I
think by another dog holding the leash in its
mouth. What happened next at first made me think
the black dog had be decapitated. What actually
happened was that the other dog had pulled on the
leash so hard that the collar came off and took
the black dogs fur and skin with it. The fur
and skin came off just like a cover off of a golf
club and now the black dog was running
around the beach with its skull completely
exposed.

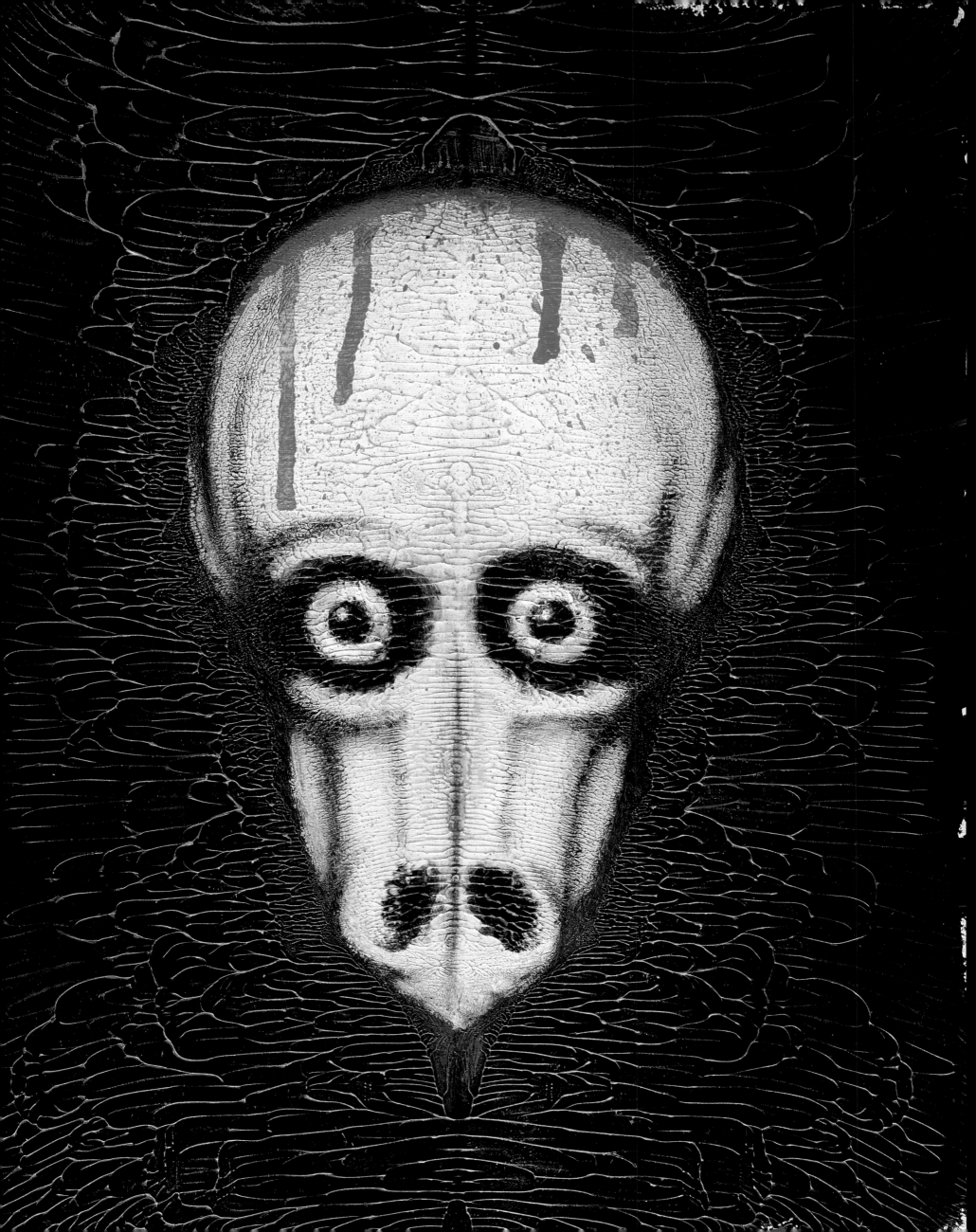

March 19, 03 L.A.

I was asked to play on stage with Fleetwood Mac. The instrument I had was made of metal and glass and a pair of shoes. The instrument was played with mallets that would be used to play a vibraphone. I was really worried because I had no idea how to play this thing. I was aware I have no musical talent and there was a huge crowd waiting for the band to come on any minute.

March 25, 03 L.A.

I don't know where I was, there was a woman who needed a ride home. There were two cars we could use, a small car and a larger ~~$~~ Ford. The woman said she felt safer on the freeway in the larger Ford. Now we were on the freeway, I was driving and everything was going well ~~or~~ when all of a sudden a car in front of me did a u-turn. There was nothing I could do to avoid smashing into the car. As I hit the breaks I woke up, my heart was pounding.

Sandra and I were driving down Runyon canyon road to
stay at a house near the bottom of the hill. When we arrived
the house we were to stay in was on fire, so we went across
the road to another house where we could spend the night.
The unusal thing about this house was that instead of a
carpet in the livingroom the room was filled with three or
four inches of wall to wall water. In the water were beautiful
turquoise fish.

April 8, 03 L.A.

I was in Baghdad standing next to the site where the Americans had dropped four bunker buster bombs the night before trying to kill Saddam Hussein. The area had been completely cleaned up in only a few hours over night. The spot where there was once a large building was now more of a vacant dirt lot than a bomb site but people were still getting ready to dig in this place, looking for the body of Saddam Hussein and his sons. Next to the bomb site was an East Indian looking statue. It had been placed there as a shrine. The gold statue of a woman or goddess type figure was on all fours with her bum sticking up in the air. Someone was asking me what I thought of the war. I said I was torn, because I felt the world would be a better place without a man like Saddam Hussein. On the other hand I still felt strongly that it was a step backwards for civilization to still be solving our world problems by going to war.

This dream was a direct result of watching the news just before I went to bed.

April 15, 03 L.A.

Jenny and I had just come back to my house after a walk. We both needed a shower, so I went to my bedroom to change out of my clothes. When I was just about completely undressed Jenny said "can I come in" I said I was not dressed and she said it didn't matter to her so I said alright. Jenny had on only a towel and when she turned around her back side wasn't covered. She wiggled her bum a little and gave me a coy look. Now we were both naked. I was standing behind her caressing her bottom with one hand and her breasts with the other hand and kissing her on the neck. Then Jenny said no we can't do this. Meaning to Sandra and David.

May 13, L.A.

Jayme and I were sleeping in a very large tent. Just outside the tent we could hear a pack of wolves. Jayme said "how cool" but as the wolves got closer and louder and seemed to be entering the tent I became very nervous but then the sprinklers came on and the wolves ran away.

April 22, 03 L.A.

Sandra and I were walking through a wood
We came upon a man running around a tree
trying to catch one of several roosters, he was having
no luck. The roosters were beautiful, with long
necks covered in bright blue feathers. I quietly came
up behind one rooster and grabbed it with great ease.
I expected the rooster to struggle but it did not. Then the
rooster turned into a dog. A good sized dog, white with
light brown patches. Normaly this dog didn't like
strangers but he became quickly attached to me. As
I held the dog, petting it and scratching its chin I
was talking to a young man at a table. The table was set
up in the woods for a funeral the next day and people were
gathering to pay their respects. As the young man told us
about the man who had passed away he was eating
caviar. He was very messy as he ate, dropping caviar all
over the table and his lap. I hated to see the waste
and wished I could have some caviar to. Sandra and I
went to sleep on the ground in the woods. I slept with
my head on the dogs hind quarters, the dog and I were
very content and a dreamed of us growing old together. Then
I heard a low soft whistle, it was the dogs owner and
the dog had to leave. The next morning the funeral group
was there. A man that looked like Jeff Bridges was telling
me that the young man I talked to was gone and I
told him that my dog had also left during the night.
But I was pleased to see that today we all had our
own jars of caviar.

May 29, 03 Barga, Italy

I was at a gas station or a roadside rest stop. For some reason people were bringing their pets to show me. I seemed to have a real way with the animals. One woman brought me her little white dog and it snuggled up under my chin. Then there was a white cat and then a black cat. The black cat was lying on its back and I was petting its stomach. Then the black cat turned into a beautiful dark haired woman.

May 29, 03 Barga, Italy

I was with Jay and David. I walked through a door that had an oval shaped window in it. In the room was a beautiful, tall, slender dark haired woman. I said if you look through that window you can see a guy that wants to ask you for a date, and I pointed to Jay through the window. At first I thought it must be like looking into a mirror with me standing next to her and Jay on the oval window. I said, "what do you think" and she said "I think I'm in love". I thought if its love at first sight why wouldn't she be in love with me? She asked if Jay knew what I was doing and I said no. Then she said "isn't that a bit cruel? and I said no, not if you go out with him. At first there may have been some confusion as to who I was pointing at because my partner Dave was with Jay and a guy that looked like carrot top.

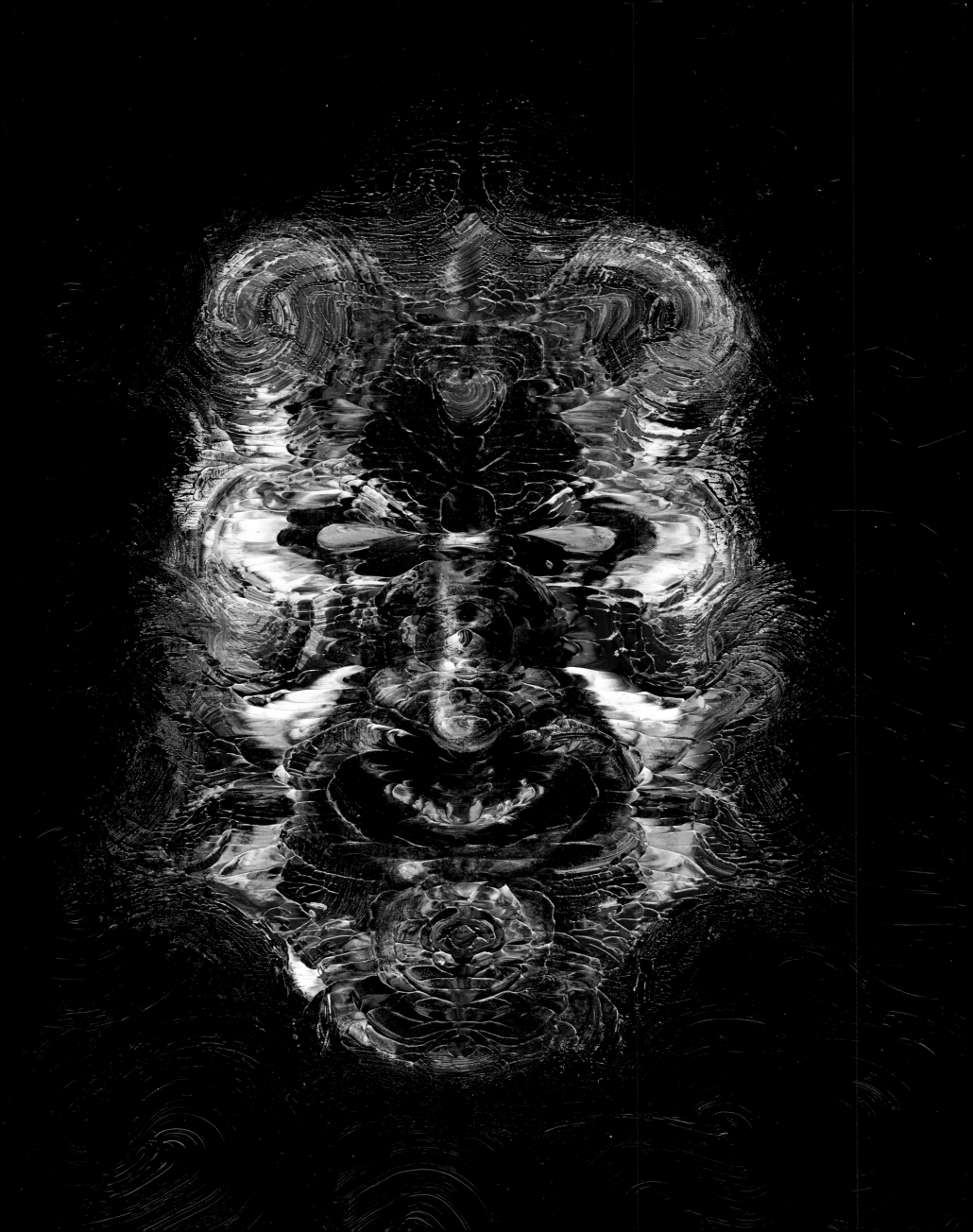

June 1, 03 Barga, Italy

I read in Communication Art magazine that the magazine was sponsoring a workshop of some kind. Then Sandra and I were in a restaurant in a train station. It was a darkish room a dark haired young woman sat across from us. Then Sandra and I were walking through the station and Sandra was mad at some people for making fun of Richard Gere singing on the Radio. Then Sandra and I were on the train platform. Sandra said I should call CA magazine for for more details. When I called a woman answered. There was some witty banter then I asked her about the workshop and there was no reply. And when I tried to say hello are you still there I had lost my voice I felt it would be rude to hang up but I had no choice, the woman from CA did not respond and couldn't.

then I am back on the platform with Sandra. I am trying to tell her how I had lost my voice but as soon as I began to explain my voice came back and Sandra gave me a look of disbelief, like oh sure. Then we were back in the restaurant our food was still on the table. As I began to eat a stew like dish of meat and vegetables I noticed that I had slopped a lot of the stew on the table around my bowl. I was embarassed to be so messy, the dark haired girl was still there and I wanted the waitress to come over so I could ask her to clean up the mess for me.

Luigi e Roberto,
Ti vedeve a presto!

VINCENT SCHIAVELLI

Vince

June 4, 03 Barga, Italy

I went over to Lindsey Buckingham's house because he had just written three new songs and I had a plan to make money with these songs. I have no idea what the plan was but in this dream it would work. I rang the bell at Lindsey's house and a roadie type guy answered the door after several rings. One look and it was obvious he and Lindsey had been up all night playing and recording music. Lindsey was not avalible so I left a message and was on my way. As I left Lindsey's house I met Judy Wong. I told her I think I want to move to San Francisco and she said why don't you move to New York, its a brand new city. Then I was in a parking lot. Jerry Wilson pulled up in a car with several other guys inside. At first I wanted to avoid him, not that I don't like him but I was in a different mental space at that moment but we made eye contact and I went over to him. We shook hands and hugged. then I remembered that I had a date with Jerry to be in a crossword puzzle contest. Together we went to find a quiet spot to plan how we would approach this team style crossword competition. Then the alarm sounded and I woke out of the deepest sleep.

June 6, 03 Barga, Italy

Sandra, Liz, Brenda and I were at a hotel somewhere in Italy. I went downstairs to the lobby just as Mick Fleetwood was entering the hotel. Mick saw me and gave me a big hug, he said he was here for Brendas birthday. Mick had cut his hair very short and shaved off his beard leaving just a mustache. He also had several large zits. He thought he looked great, I thought he looked pretty bad. I also thought how would Fleetwood Mac fans ever recognise him? Then Brenda came down to the lobby and Mick gave her a big hug and a kiss.

Mick and I were now out walking on the streets of a big city. A beautiful young woman was walking towards us, Mick and I looked at eachother, he was going to try out his new look and I indicated "go for it." He walked up to her, slapped her on the ass and kissed her. It turns out she was a hooker and didn't mind at all. Then I noticed we had wandered into an area of the city where people had sex in the street all the time. There were lines of men fucking women, women fucking men with dildos, women giving men blow jobs, men giving men blow jobs. The whole scene looked very dirty and didn't appeal to me. As I walked away I could see Mick standing in line getting a blow job.

MUSEO DELLA FIGURINA DI GESSO E DELL'EMIGRAZIONE

Palazzo Vanni - Via del Mangano, 17
Tel. (0583) 78082

INGRESSO

13519

Comune di Coreglia Antelmine''i (Lucca)

-Barga-

CHIUSO SABATO A COLAZIONE E DOMENICA

OSTERIA

St. ANA

00186 Roma
Via della Penna, 68/69
(continuazione Via dell'Oca)
Tel. 06/36.10.291
Fax 06/32.13.521

June 14, 03 Rome, Italy

Dave had organized a kind of weekend retreat at a place in the hills above Malibu. It was not easy to get to, Sandra and I had to use her old 4runner and drive off road. When we got there Dave was nowhere to be found. The place seemed crowded and I didn't really know what was going on. I met a young dark haired woman, she was rather plain looking but very nice. We walked and ~~tai~~ talked and I asked her how she liked living in this small town. She said "Don't ever move to a small town". I went to an information booth and asked someone I thought was a girl if she had information about Dave ~~Ellis~~ but when I looked down I saw the person was not wearing pants and I could see his penis. I finally saw Sandra again, I think she had seen Dave but was still confused so we went back to the information booth but it was now a hotdog stand. Sandra and I wanted to leave but now found ourselves on a roof and ~~~~ more confused.

June 20, 03 L.A.

I was at a very expensive restaurant with Jay and Margo. Margo was looking slender and had collagen in ~~the~~ her lips. Jay and Margo came here often and Margo knew all of the waiters by their first name. We were eating caviar and potatos au gratin. Then Margo was giving a hard time to Jeri Hall, who was sitting next to me. I thought, wow Margo gives shit to everybody. Then Jay and Margo went into another room and Jeri Hall had moved her table away from me and was now dining with a friend. Then waiter removed my plate before I had finished my caviar. ~~#~~ I told the waiter I still had half a portion of caviar on my plate and I thought he would be right back but instead he sat down to his own dinner. Margo came back to the table and said Jay went home because he had a cold. Then there was a green fire truck in the room and as it went by it almost smashed our table.

July 12, 03 L.A.

I was riding in a convertable with Peter Morton. We were in a beach town and he was talking about a 4 year window of opportunity on a real estate deal. He said "Wait till they see Malibu and there will be no stopping them". For some reason I was peeing in my pants (tennis shorts) and hoped they would dry before we reached wherever we were going. It was a beautiful sunny day.

July 13, 03 L.A.

Kevin Costner was an outlaw in the old west. He had just been captured and was lying in bed in a hotel room. Sitting in a chair next to him on his right was the sheriff and standing to Kevin's left were two deputies, one was Ward Bond. The sheriff asked Kevin for his gun and said, "can we be reasonable about this"? Kevin smiled and removed the pearl handle gun from its holster using his fingertips. As a deputy reached for the gun Kevin moved it just out of his reach, the deputy reached again and Kevin once again teased him. The sheriff gave the deputies a look as he drew his gun and shot Kevin twice in the chest. Now Kevin was Kirk Douglas, an old Kirk Douglas with white hair. He got up from the bed and was staggering, a deputy punched him and threw him up against the wall. Kirk staggered back and even though he was basically dead on his feet he said "how can we solve this"? and Ward Bond said "with genoside" as he hit Kirk again with a mighty blow to the face.

July 22, 03 L.A.

I dreamed that Mary Pastor died.

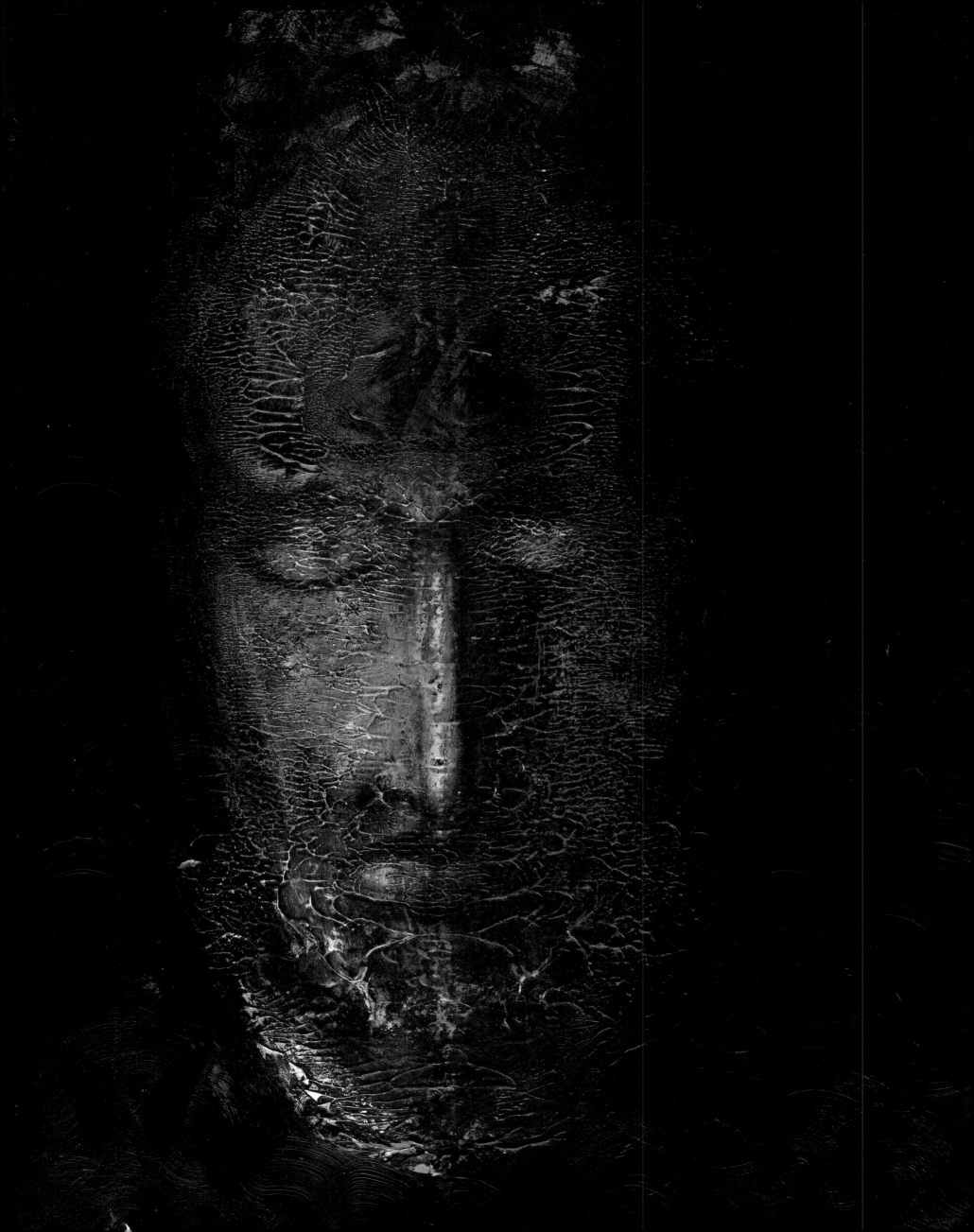

Aug 3, 03 L.A.

David and I were sitting on the beach watching the surfers. There was one guy getting a very good ride but he didn't pull out of the wave at the right time and he got caught in a very strong shore break. We could see him tumbling with his surfboard in the tube of the wave. The wave hit the shore with thundering force and the surfer was left lying on the sand. Dave said he has to be dead, I ran over to see what I could do. The surfer was wrapped in a towel that went around him and the board. It was a white towel and he looked like someone you would see at an Indian funeral. I unwrapped the towel enough to see his face. His eyes were open but he looked very dead. I said, somebody get a lifeguard. Then I looked behind me and saw another huge wave about to break on me and everyone else gathered around the surfer. I knew we would be tossed together as if in a washing machine. Then I woke up, it was very scary.

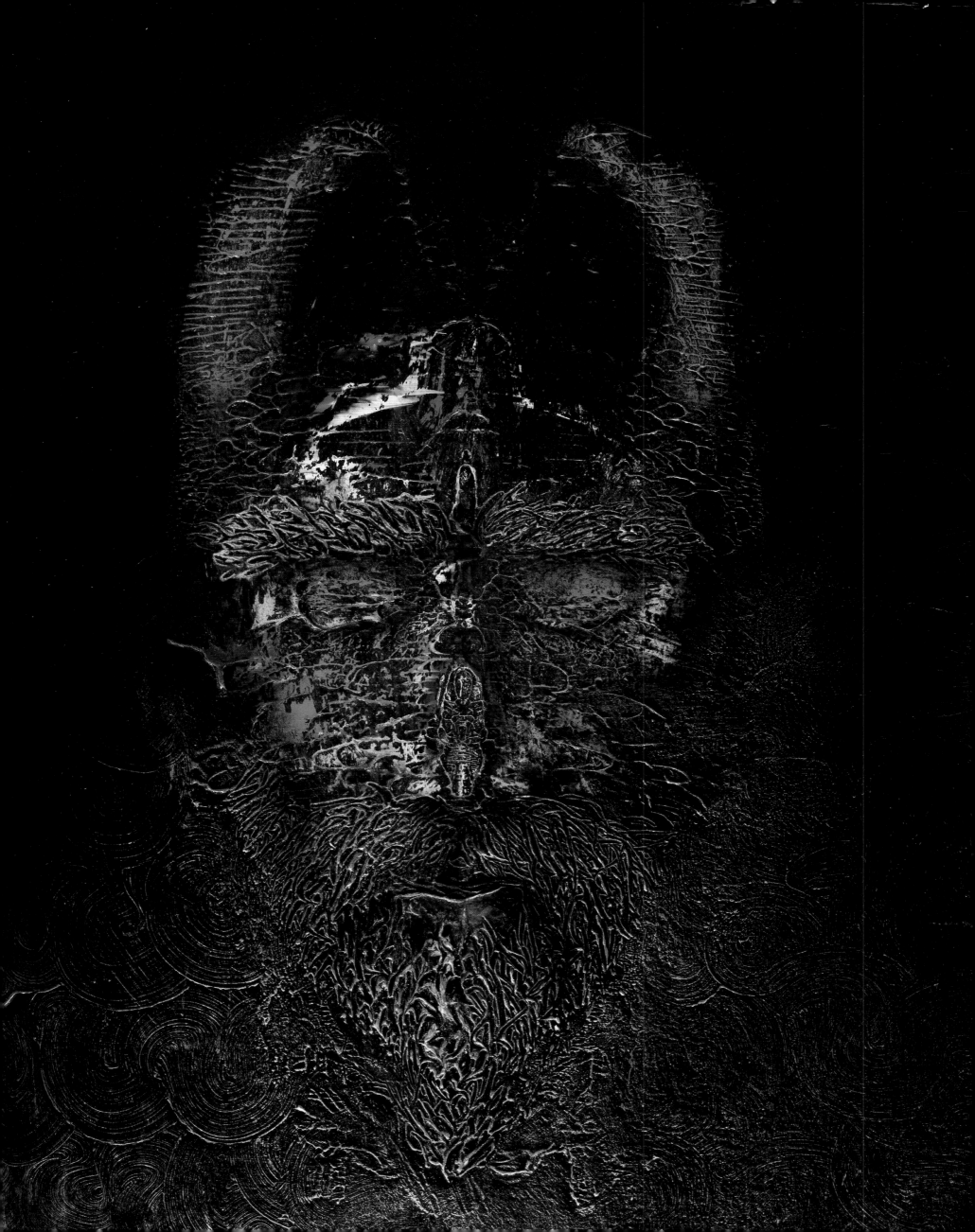

Aug. 19, 03 L.A.

I was living in an ~~apt~~ apartment in the Sycamore ave, La Brea area. I was working on some paintings similar to the one on the page to the right. At some point in the painting process I put the art work in the oven and went out for a walk in the neighborhood. I had put on a pair of very expensive shoes I had purchased in San Francisco many years ago for $400. I had not put the shoes on correctly and my heels were not all the way in the shoes. It was difficult to walk this way but I thought it would be ok for a short stroll. Then I came upon a police crime scene. There were several squad cars ~~with~~ with their lights flashing and a lot of activity. An apartment building was cordoned off with the yellow police tape and there was a pole stuck in

the ground with a sign attached to it that read rope scene. Then I remembered my art work at home in the oven, but now it was food in the oven not my paintings. I thought I have to have some wine with my meal, so I had better go to the market and buy some before I go home. I put my expensive dress shoes on correctly and began to walk quickly or run down the street to get my wine and go home.

Aug 25, 03 L.A.

I was sitting in a restaurant when my dad walked in. He looked great, he had both of his legs and seemed very healthy. He was wearing a beautiful gray suit and a white shirt but no tie. I said, "wow! its great to see you, I haven't see you for a long time." I said I have really missed you and he said he had really missed me too. Then we hugged a very loving hug.

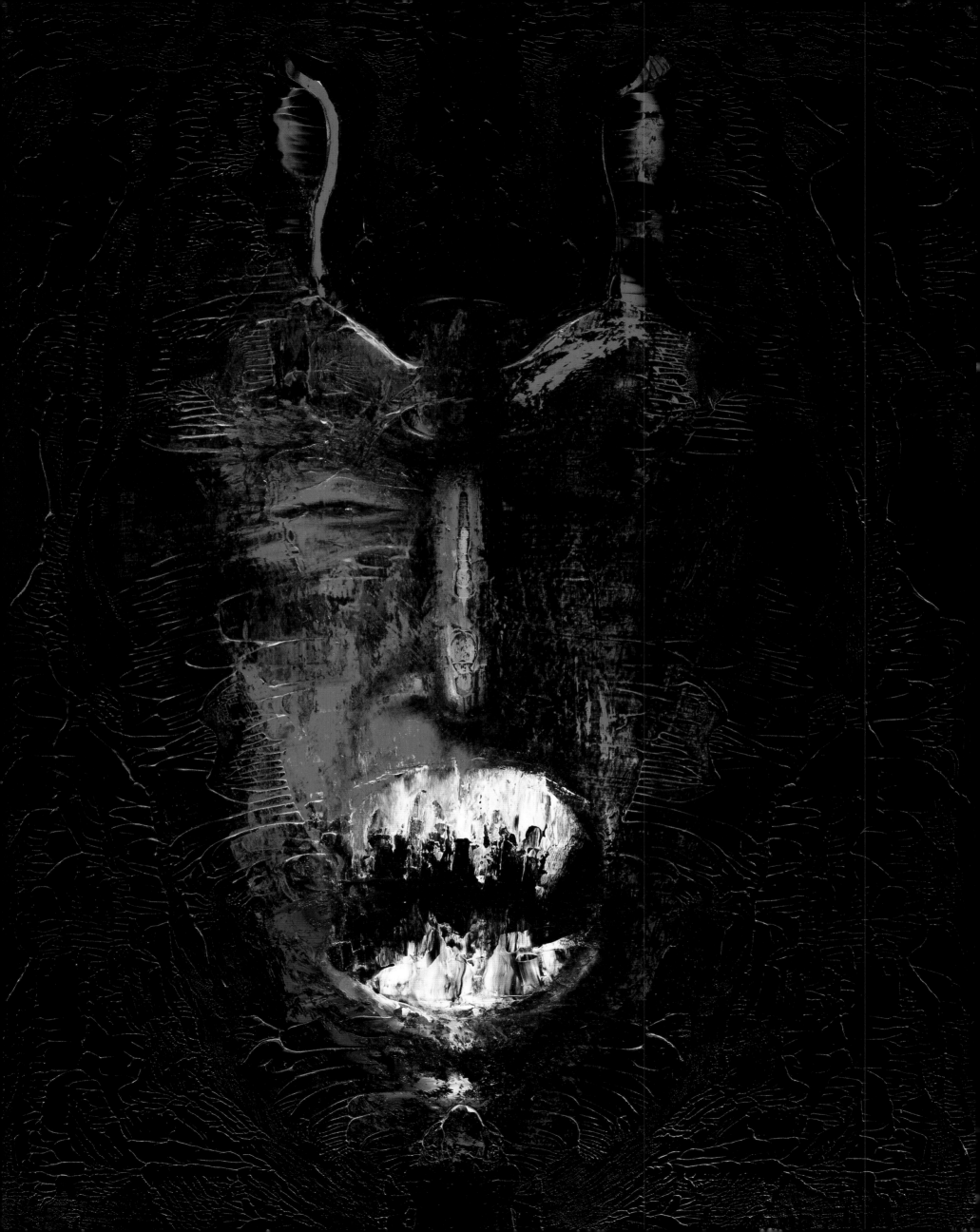

Aug. 20, 03 L.A.

Vigon/Ellis was moving into new offices. It was an older building with some good character. There was a lot of activity going on inside. There were workmen working away and old employees like Marissa and Malissa were moving furniture. There was a large area for designers to work, a conference room a large bathroom and two identical office each with a fireplace, one for me and one for Dave. The new place was on the second floor of a two story building, there were plenty of windows so there was no shortage of good light and views of the neighborhood. Then for some reason I shit my pants. I was a little panicked at first but quickly went into the bathroom. I shut the door and was relieved to see that there was a very good lock on the door so I was assured of privacy. The mess was quite small and easy to clean up. I wanted to sit on the toilet but where the seat was attached there was a small water leak at the hinges. I blotted at the point of the leak for a long time and I was finally able to sit down on the toilet. As I sat there I saw a tiny little man with a big head walk across the bathroom floor. He was no taller than an inch and he was translucent blue and thin like a sheet of paper or plastic. Then another man even smaller was dancing across the floor. I couldn't see any of his features he was just the shape of a man with very delicate limbs.

Sept 14, 03 L.A.

I was at Brian and Anahit's home for dinner. The other guests were Anahit's mom and my brother Jay. There was a lot of great Middle Eastern food. After dinner my brother went to sleep in the guest room and Brian went to bed in another guest room because their dog peed on the bed in his room. As the sun came up I wanted to get some sleep, but because all of the rooms were taken I had no choice but to get into bed with Jay.

Sept 20, 03 L.A.

I was driving my silver Mercedes on a city street when some external force maybe a strong wind caused my car to flip over onto its roof. I got out of the car, I wasn't hurt and to my surprise I was able to easily flip the car right side up all by myself.

Oct 14, 03 L. A.

I woke up this morning and felt something funny in my left ear. I reached up and pulled an old used tea bag out of my ear and threw it on the floor because it seemed so creepy. Then I picked it up to take a closer look at it. The tea bag had a price tag on it. I examined the price tag more closely, not to see the price but to see if there was a date on the tag so I could tell how long it had been in my ear.

Oct. 24, 03 L A

There were three holes in the bedroom carpet. The holes were all the way through to the wooden floor. I had no idea how the holes got there and the carpet was too new to be worn out.

Oct. 31, 03 L.A.

I was in Mexico with my partner David.
We were sitting at a round table in a
plaza. There was some kind of festival
going on. A beautiful young Mexican girl
sat down next to me. We were flirting with
each other and holding hands. It turned
out that she was a prostitute. We decided
to go back to her place. When we arrived at
her place I had to pee. I went into the
bathroom, it was a room with just a
toilet and a mirror. As I was peeing I could
see myself in the mirror. For some reason
I was wearing a loose fitting sleevless
~~~~ T-shirt, my body looked great like ~~~
~~~~~~ like in a photo from the cover of
Mens Fitness magazine. The beautiful Mexican
girl was watching me as I was peeing. She
liked the way I looked and really wanted to
get into bed with me and the fact that I
was 54 years old didn't matter. Then something happend and we couldn't get right into
bed. The next thing I remember was going
back to her place to find her and continue where
we ~ left off. I remember finding her but
then I woke up. I spoke Italian and she
spoke Mexican but we had no problem understanding each other.

Nov. 9. 03 L.A.

I was driving behind Brian. I don't know where we were going but Brian was leading the way. Brian had a GPS in his car but he could not make heads nor tails of the system. We came to a stop and I got into Brian's car to take over driving and navigation but we still could not figure out where we were going.

Nov. 22, 03 L.A.

I was in my car, Flossy was with me. She was young and healthy. Sandra called me in the car and asked me to pick up some bread on the way home. I drove to Fairfax and Flossy and I walked up the street to find a bakery. Flossy was very content walking on the leash just ahead of me. We came to a bakery and Deli, I tied Flossy up outside and went in. I couldn't get any service. I saw Flossy through the glass door, she was off her leash. When I went outside I saw that she had chewed through her leash. She did not want to be alone on the street. I went to tie the leash to her collar, she rolled over a little nervous. I rubbed her tummy and told her how beautiful a little girl she was. We walked some more and came to the remains of a chopped down bush. A three foot high twig like trunk. Flossy jumped up on top of the trunk, there was just enough room for he four little paws. Then she began to pee but not a normal pee but like a small hose almost fountain like.

Nov. 24, 03 L.A.

I saw Troy at the gym. He looked terrible. He told me that he had been very sick and that he was not yet fully recovered.

Nov. 28, 03 L.A.

I was with my brother but it was not my brother. He was older and bigger and did not look like a twin. He and his girlfriend were bank robbers. They had been on the lam for a long time and knew they were about to be caught. I was in a public bathroom with my brother, I think talking about his immanent arrest. He asked me for some toilet paper but there was none to be found anywhere in the bathroom. Then he was driving me home up the hill from the valley. He said he was sorry for my envolvement in his life of crime. My use of criminal lingo was very good. Then he said, "I never saw Jung die." Meaning there was no doubt he was dead but just that he hadn't seen it.

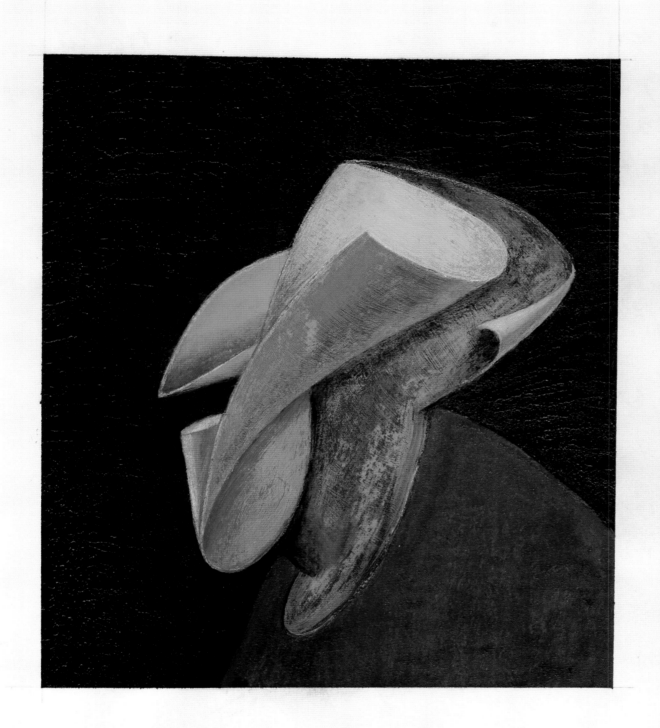

Dec. 14, 03 L.A.

I was walking down the street in Hollywood. I was going to the Chinese theater to see a movie. I was on Franklin Ave. when Sandra walked by but didn't notice me. I had to call to her three times before she turned around. She was preoccupied with something and she was being a little mysterious. She finally told me that she had taken a job as a fortune teller.

Dec. 14, 03 L.A.

I was walking into a restaurant. I was carrying Flossy with my left arm, she was curled up nose to bottom. The restaurant had a Polynesian theme. A waiter showed me to a table all the way in the back of the restaurant. As the waiter left he gave a funny look at Flossy. When I went to put Flossy down on the booth seat she was stiff as a board, like she was having a seizure. Then as soon as I put her down and gave her a little pat she came out of it bright eyed and healthy.

I had this same exact dream twice today, once this morning and again during an afternoon nap.

Dec. 16, 03 L.A.

I was having dinner at the Beverly Hills Hotel with Emma Thompson and David Jones. I said to Emma, I had a dream last night about this exact dinner. Just then Judy Wong sat down at the table behind me. She leaned over and said ~~~ dinner with Linda Thompson and I said no, Emma Thompson. Emma and David seemed to be attracted to eachother. They left the restaurant and I was leaving when Steve Martin stopped me and said, lets have a fake gun fight. He walked a few paces, turned and with his fingers made a gun like gesture. I also made a gun like gesture and beat him to the draw. Steve made a very dramatic death scene. He was sprawled out on the restaurant floor. I walked over and kicked one of his feet, blew on my finger as if it were a smoking gun and put in an imaginary holster, then walked away. As I was leaving the hotel I met Pierce Brosnon, there was some small talk and I left. I found David Jones's car keys in my pocket and figured that Emma had her own car. I went home but returned to the hotel a short time later to try and find David. I went to the hotel bar and ran into Pierce again. He said, are you still here? Arnold Schwarzenegger was at the bar, drunk out of his mind. He stumbled over to me and threw his arms around me, I had to hold him up. Pierce and I tied up Arnold and put him on a bench in front of the hotel. Someone had called the police so Pierce and I walked away leaving Arnold on the bench. As I walked back to the hotel I remembered that Keith Bright had the hotel gift shop as a client but lost the account.

Dec. 16, 03 L.A.

I was hanging out with Mick Jagger. We seemed to be good friends. I asked him something about his house and he said "why don't you come over and you can see what I've done with it."

Now I am at Mick's house. The house is very plain and small, no art on the walls, not at all what I had expected. Mick said come here I want to show you something. It was an album cover for a new recording he had just completed with the Blues Brothers. There was a photo of John Belushi and Dan Aykroyd but no photo of Mick on the package. There was a full bleed photo of Belushi on the front and a full bleed of Aykroyd on the back. The photos were in color and had an interesting grainy quality.

Then I was in my bed. I felt someone pushing on my shoulder. I was half awake but I could not wake up and I could not figure out where I was. Then I saw Jay, he was the one pushing me. He was on the bed, on his knees with his arms above his head ready to strike me on the head. I woke up just before he could hit me.

January 4, 04 L.A.

Jay and I were in the military. It was our night off and we were waiting in line with a lot of other guys waiting to see some prostitutes. As I stood in line I remembered I had cut my penis in half in a dream I had the night before. I kept trying to stick it back together before it was my turn to see one of the girls. Every time I tried to put my cock in place I thought it looked funny and if anything sexual were to happen it would fall apart immediately. Then it was my turn to see one of the girls and there I was holding the top half of my cock in my left hand. Once in the room I saw the girl, she was a young dark haired slender type and quite attractive. I told her there was something wrong with my cock, that it had been cut in half during a fight. Just as I told her that story I looked down and saw that my cock was completely normal, good as new and added "but its fine now."

Now we are both naked and we are kissing, then I am kissing her breasts. Her skin is smooth and soft and she smells wonderful. Then I notice she is laughing a kind of bored laugh and I say "whats wrong"? and she says its always the same old thing with all the guys. I asked her what I could do that was different and she said "come back a few times and I'll show you". I said, "but I haven't come yet" and she said "don't focus on that so much come back and see me and I'll show you things you have never seen before."

Then I was outside of the whore house, laying on top of a truck wrapped in a blanket. Then there was a lot of noise and activity going on in the parking lot where

I am ontop of the truck. Now I realize the whorehouse is in a fenced in compound guarded by a large police force. The police have just caught two of the prostitutes I guess who were trying to get away. They hit th girls and threw them on the ground. Then one of the policemen broke both legs of one girl and the foot of the other girl. Now I was worried they might think I was some kind of a trouble maker, so I climbed down off the truck and tried to make my way to the exit. It was dificult to make any progress because it seemed that the entire compound had erupted into a riot situation.

January 12, 04 L.A.

I was in bed reading a book. Norman was sitting in a chair to my left. There was a light in the ceiling and two worms hung from the light by some kind of thread. One worm lowered itself down close to my face and I took a swing at it with the book I was reading but the worm quickly moved up towards the light to avoid my swing. This happened again and the third time it happened Norman said "you know I've had some great conversations with those creatures." Then I got out of bed and cupped one of the worms in my hands and gently shook the worm. As I shook the worm it turned into a large white flower, then the flower flew around the room and fell apart over the bed. Next I cupped the other worm in my hands, gently shook it and it turned into a large red flower, flew around the room and fell apart over the bed. When the flowers fell apart they let off an intoxicating gas and if you were asleep and breathed in this gas you could have wonderful conversations with the flowers.

January 18, 04 L.A.

Sandra and I were in a house with my father. He was healthy and looked good with both his legs, he even dressed well. The odd thing was that every time he saw me he called me Nelly. I said "do you call me Nelly because you miss her"? Dad replied, "No, I didn't have enough money to save her. Before he said this he had to think about my question for a minute.

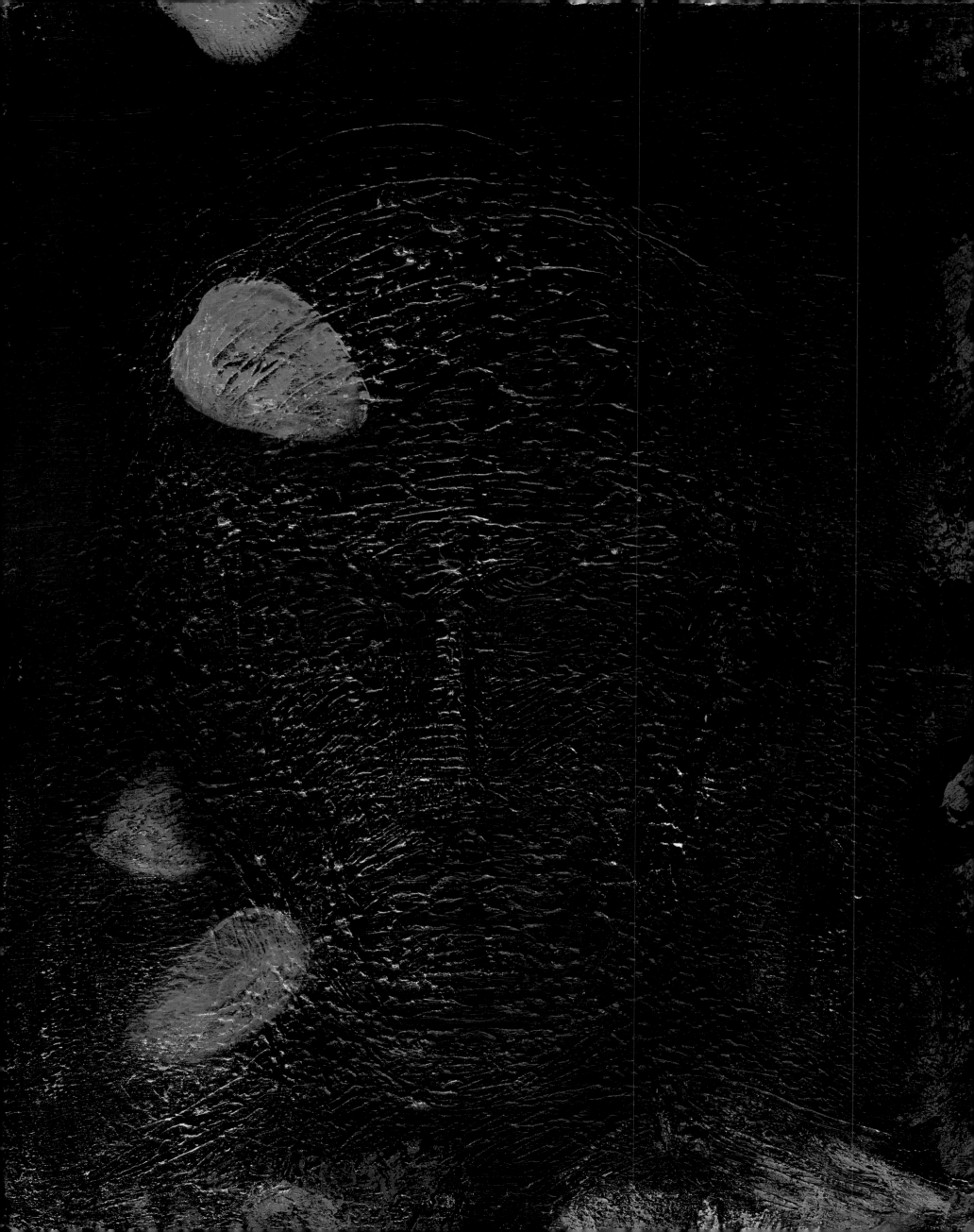

Feb 8, 04 L.A.

Sandra and I were living on a large farm.
It seemed to have hundreds of acres. It was a
beautiful peaceful setting that one day was invaded
by a film crew or some big production, entertainment
type group. In a field I met a beautiful young black
girl. She was with a white girl about her same age. The
black girl invited me to have sex with the both of them
but I said no, I'm married. The black girl said, "how
long have you been married?" I told her 26 years and
she said "wow," "how have you lasted so long together? I
said by being able to say no to beautiful girls like
you. I think we laughed. Then I went off alone with
the black girl. We were in town, there were lots of
people around. The whole time we were together she kept
trying to get me to have sex with her. Finally I gave
in. I saw her naked as she went into a portable toilet,
her body was perfect. Then we were on a sofa, but the
sofa was in public, she was giving me a blow job
even though other people were watching. Then I realized
that I had been gone all day and I had to explain
to Sandra my whereabouts for the day. ~~I~~ I told
the beautiful black girl I had to go. She said "OK
but you have to fuck me tommorow." I was thinking,
great but how do I keep Sandra ~~f~~ from suspecting
that something is going on.

February 16, 04 L.A.

I was at the doctors office for a regular checkup. Bob Carbone was there ahead of me. Then it was my turn. I was wearing one of those doctor office gowns. I was sitting on the examination table when a woman doctor came in to do the exam. She said she wanted to examine my penis while my gown was open. She said my penis had to be hard for the exam so she started sucking my cock. I was surprised and wondered if the other doctors and nurses did this. The doctor said this was the way she knew best and I said "there are other ways."

February 21, 04 L.A.

Sandra and I were in bed. Sandra was asleep but she was making strange noises like the Linda Blair character in the Exorcist. I kicked her and she stopped but began talking. I don't know what she was saying but then she started making that strange sound again. It's a good thing I was sleeping with my back to Sandra because in my dream I kicked at her so hard I woke myself up.

March 31, 04 L.A.

I was with Scott Griffith. We were in a very large run down warehouse. Scott said, "did you hear that Noel Coward died?" I said no, but he must have been very old. Scott replied yes, one hundred seventeen. We both had to use the bathroom. As we entered the filthy bathroom a man passed us on his way out. In the bathroom were maybe five toilets in wooden stalls. None of the stalls had doors and there were no urinals. Scott went into a stall and I went into the one next to him. The toilet in my stall had a strange mobile like sculpture sticking out of it, I wondered if I could make it move by peeing on it. Then I heard a couple of plopping sounds from the stall next to me and I knew Scott had to do more than just pee.

April 4, 04 L.A.

David and I were at my house. We were walking down the hallway from the livingroom towards the bedroom when a hummingbird landed on my sleeve. When I tried to ~~catch~~ catch it the bird flew into my hair. David said, "here let me get it you don't want a hummingbird in your hair." I said, "no I don't mind." Then the hummingbird started to peck at my scalp and I laughed. I went into the guest bedroom to look into a mirror. I removed the bird from my hair and held it in my right hand, it was beautiful. I let the bird go but instead of flying away it flew into the sunglasses I ~~was~~ wearing. Once again I held the hummingbird in my hand but this time I took it outside before I let it go.

The following Wednesday I found a hummingbird nest on my patio. It had been blown out of a tree. The next Saturday I found this hummingbird on another part of the patio. It had flown into a window.

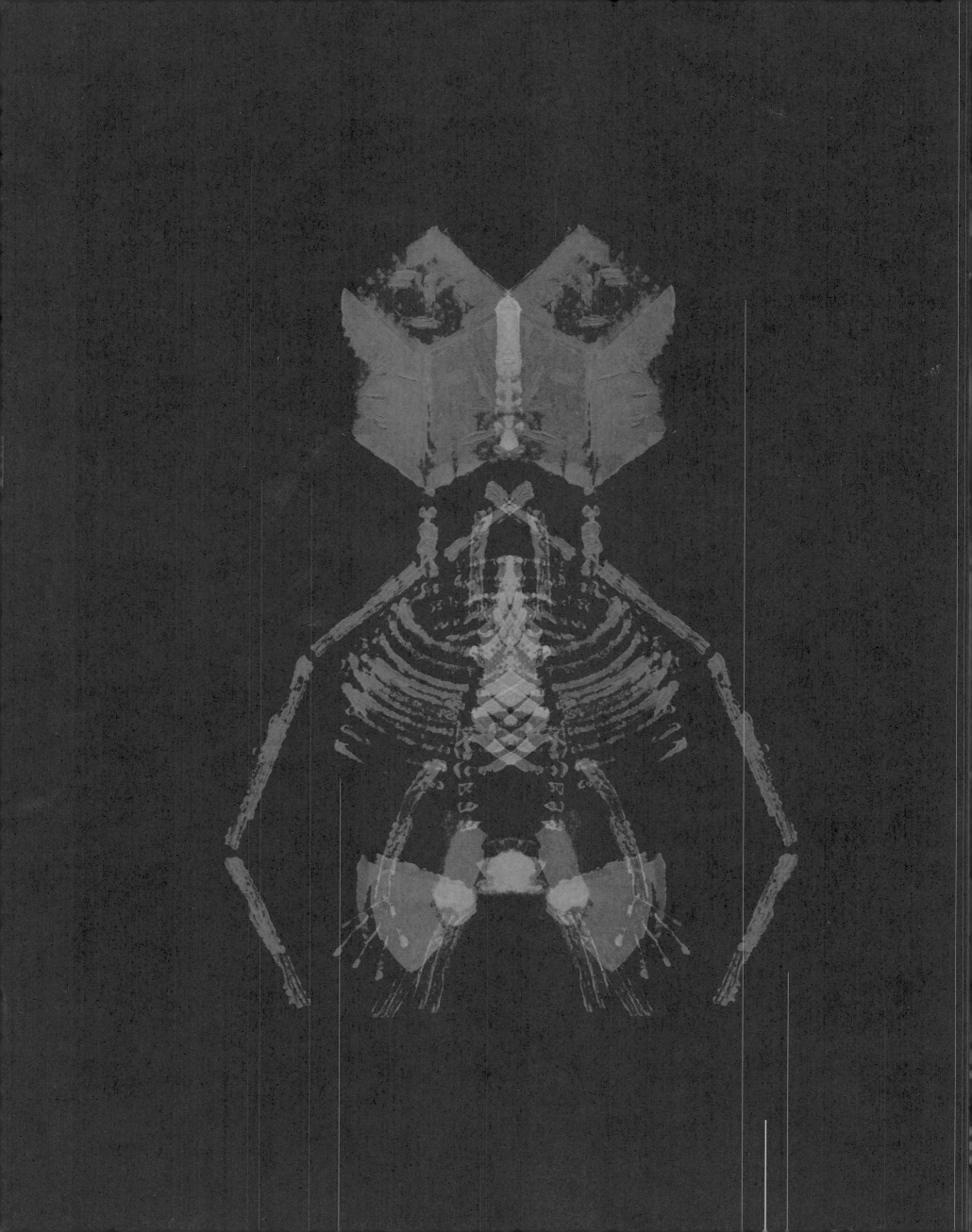